KU-167-500

Whisky

The Water of Life

Whisky

The Water of Life

MARGARET BRIGGS

LOMOND

© Copyright 2009 Bookmart Limited

All rights reserved.
No part of this publication may be reproduced, stored
in a retrieval system or transmitted by any means,
electronic, mechanical, photocopying or otherwise,
without the prior permission in writing
of the publisher.

ISBN 978-1-84204-185-7

1 3 5 7 9 10 8 6 4 2

This edition published in 2009 for
Lomond Books Ltd, Broxburn, Scotland
www.lomondbooks.com

Produced by Omnipress Limited, UK
Cover design by Omnipress Limited, UK

Printed in Dubai

THE AUTHOR
MARGARET BRIGGS was a teacher for 30 years, working
in Kent, Germany, North Yorkshire and Sussex. Since
leaving teaching she has embarked on a second career
as a freelance writer, researcher and editor, alongside
her writer husband, Lol. Margaret has written a
number of best selling books in the series (including
Vinegar, Porridge, Honey, Ginger, Bicarbonate of Soda
and others). Margaret has adopted a new approach in
exploring and researching these subjects, previously
considered to be the preserve of the connoisseur or
expert. The results are books which all readers find
informative and entertaining.

CONTENTS

INTRODUCTION

Whisky is an ancient Celtic drink made from a few simple ingredients and has been in existence for hundreds of years, in one form or another. Whisky, or whiskey as it is spelt in some countries, is a general term for a range of distilled drinks, so we need to be more specific. I suppose it's a bit like calling all drinks produced from grapes, wine.

The infinite variability and complexities that different forms of the spirit offer are something else, or so I've been told. I have to come clean and profess my novice status on the subject of whisky tasting, but I am quite aware of the difference between single malt and a blend. I also know that it can relieve stress, remove inhibitions or fire up passion. It can slip down the throat easily but come back to haunt you unmercifully the next day.

It's funny to note that nowadays Scotch whisky is more popular out of Scotland than at home, and is sold in around 200 countries. Whisky consumption makes a great contribution to the tax revenue of countries all over the world. Whisky is big business. The method of producing whiskies in such diverse countries as Canada, Ireland, the US, India and Japan isn't all that different, even if the taste is.

Purists would be horrified by the idea of mixing whisky with ice or soda, cola or ginger ale, but whether you mix it or knock it back neat or as a chaser after a pint, as in many Scottish pubs, there are many ways to enjoy it. You can even cook with it, if allowed!

This book isn't for the self anointed whisky connoisseurs, but for people like me who'd like to know a little about the background, origins and make up of one of the greatest uses of malt and barley in the world. It's the greatest invention since porridge!

WHAT IS WHISKY?

WHAT IS WHISKY?

Let's start off with a few definitions and explanations of spelling variations. If you are buying Scotch *whisky* there is an obvious difference in spelling from Irish *whiskey*. If you talk about whisky to most people they will think of Scotland. Some may then distinguish between blended whisky and single malt. Apart from one brand of Irish whiskey and some American bourbons, I must admit to knowing very little about other types of the spirit before starting research on the subject.

The name whisky or whiskey comes from Gaelic, as you might imagine. *Uisge beatha* means 'water of life'. Scotland chose to lose the 'e' while the Irish kept it. In the US, the more common spelling is whiskey, whereas Canada and Japan, both producers of their own spirit, call it whisky.

The main ingredients are malted grain, yeast and water. There's a big clue in the phrases 'malt whisky' or 'single malt', although I'd not made the connection between milky malt drinks, extracts and vinegars until recently. Malt sounds so wholesome, so how can it be anything but good for you? It also makes brewing whisky more effective.

To be defined as whisky, the spirit must contain at least 40% alcohol by volume (abv). It must also have been matured in oak barrels for at least three years. In 1909, there was a failed attempt to define Scotch as being only the product of Scottish barley, although most grain is still home grown.

WHAT ARE THE INGREDIENTS FOR SCOTCH?

The germination of barley to create malt is a key factor in the finished product. Malt whisky is produced in batches, where the only ingredients are malted barley, yeast and water. You can make whisky from other grains and from malted barley in a continuous fermenting process, but this cannot be called malt. Barley ferments quite easily with yeast because of the sugars produced, and also produces a great flavour.

BARLEY
The choice of barley used is not that important, as long as the grain is of a high quality. Around 20% of the barley produced is suitable for malting. The cask used to mature the spirit seems to have a greater significance in the process. Unlike wine making, where the type or blend of grapes used is of fairly major importance (although, of course, there are a lot more factors involved in making good wine), the barley undergoes such a change during malting and distillation that the origin of the barley won't make a discernable difference in tasting tests. Some distillers believe otherwise, however, and insist on certain strains for their whisky. Leading modern strains include Golden Promise, which has been around since about 1960 and produces high yields and early harvests. This variety has declined in recent years, however, and varieties such as Prisma and Chariots are now widely used.

WHERE DOES THE GRAIN COME FROM?
A lot of grain for Scotch whisky is grown locally in Scotland, on the east coast. Imported grain can come from anywhere. Before the EU, maize was imported for grain whisky from far and wide, including South Africa and the US. Now, mostly wheat is used and

distillers insist that there is no difference in flavour. New strains of wheat have been produced which have adapted to the northern climate, and over 50% of grain is grown in Scotland. This wheat is quite different from that used to make flour and bread.

WATER

Water is essential for several reasons. You need:

- Cold water to steep the barley before malting
- Hot water for mixing with ground grain, or grist, to make the wash
- Water to cool hot, alcoholic vapours in the still and condense back to liquid. Originally, this was done with cool air, but cold water increases the yield and presumably speeds up the process.
- Demineralised water for diluting the strength to 63.5% by volume before pouring it into casks. This is the best percentage for maturing whisky.
  A higher percentage slows down the ageing process and a lower one may lead to a final percentage of less than 40, when it wouldn't be classified as whisky at all.

Clean water is essential for making good whisky and you need lots of it. So Scotland has a key natural resource and ingredient all in one. The climate and geomorphology give rise to cool mountain springs, which have proven perfect for supplying stills, soaking barley and cooling stills over centuries. Many distilleries take their water from the same burn that fed the plant originally – maybe 50 years ago. Untreated water is often regarded as an important element in the final product. Different rocks and vegetation also have a part to play in the taste of the water. See Scotland's Geology, page 56.

A modern whisky distillery can use up to 50 million litres (11 million gallons) of water per week. For cooling purposes, some of this water can be taken from rivers and later returned. It has been estimated that around 900 billion litres (198 billion gallons) of rain fall in Scotland each year and that, from this rainfall, 9 million litres (1,979,723 gallons) of whisky are produced. With a fairly constant supply of rainwater throughout the year, burns, lochs and rivers don't have time to stagnate and any bacteria resulting from the occasional sheep falling in and getting washed away are quickly rinsed out as well.

The whisky producing regions of Scotland would seem to have plenty of good-quality water at their fingertips, although water sources today are jealously guarded and many disputes over the years have resulted from water use. Distillers often buy up land to protect water sources, which can be seasonal. After a couple of warmer winters in recent years and less snowfall in the Grampians, there has been a concern about supplies. Modern industry relies on continuous production, rather than the winter/spring production of the past. This has led to an increased interest in supplies from springs and the time it takes for snow meltwater to feed into burns. Water diviners and geologists are now employed by some distillers. With climate change, drought could cause a shutdown of the production plant. Most grain today has already been malted before it reaches the distillery, with the exception of a few producers such as Bowmore, who still malt some barley on site.

DOES THE WATER AFFECT THE TASTE OF THE WHISKY?

At fermentation level the answer is yes; the water is added to the grist for mashing. Many distillers claim that the best whisky comes from soft water, namely water that has passed through peat growing over granite, although only about a fifth of Scottish distilleries come into this category.

The effect of different water on whisky making is still a fairly unknown variable. This seems quite surprising to me. I would have thought that there were a number of PhD studies just waiting to be carried out by willing students. However, geologists have recently made some very pertinent observations regarding age of rocks and water sources. See Scotland's Geology, page 56.

YEAST

It has long been recognised that different strains of yeast are best for different jobs. Yeast occurs naturally, and the first distillers probably relied on wind-borne spores. In the right conditions — warm, damp and covered — yeast cells quickly get to work on sugars or other carbohydrates. Any strain of *Saccharomyces*, especially *S. cerevisiae*, will reproduce by budding. Yeast is a froth consisting of yeast cells together with carbon dioxide, which they produce in the process of fermentation. Added to fruit juices or other substances, it produces alcoholic beverages. The yeast used to leaven bread is another type.

Different producers have their own favourite types of yeast but, generally, these are distiller's yeast or brewer's yeast. While both convert sugars into alcohol, brewer's yeast is used to add flavour during this reaction. After about 48 hours of action, the temperature and strength of alcohol kills off the yeast.

TYPES OF WHISKY

There are three main categories of whisky. These are malt, grain and blended whisky.

MALT WHISKY — Also called Pure Malt and Blended Malt, this is produced from 100% malted barley, fermented with yeast and distilled in traditional pot stills. No other grain material is allowed. Read more about it in the next section. Malt whisky from one distillery may be blended with other malts.

SINGLE MALT WHISKY — Single malt whisky is the product from one single distillery, which has not been blended with whisky from any other distillery.

SINGLE CASK SINGLE MALT — You can't get more exclusive than this: all bottles are taken from the same cask. This type of whisky is obviously going to be a lot rarer, because you only get about 300 bottles from a barrel. However, quality may vary from one cask to the next quite considerably, so you can't always guarantee the taste will be the same as a previous barrel, or what you are expecting.

GRAIN WHISKIES — Whisky can also be produced from unmalted barley as well as wheat, maize and rye, but these must always be mixed with some malted barley, which helps fermentation. As I said before, malt whisky is made in batches, whereas grain whisky can be made in a continuous process. Fermented wash is poured down a collection of tall containers at very high pressure. The liquid is vaporised and then passes against plates where it condenses again into liquid — a bit like a mini water cycle. This form of spirit has less taste than malt whisky.

SINGLE GRAIN WHISKY — This is a grain whisky from one distillery. It doesn't mean it has been made from a single type of grain, but that a single distillery has made it from malted barley and other grains.

BLENDED WHISKIES — Most whiskies sold are a blend of grain whiskies combined with about a third share of malt whiskies from, maybe, several different distilleries. Blends aim to suit the tastes and wallets of as many people as possible. Blending was introduced in the 19th century because many of the malt whiskies were too robust for the average whisky drinker. There can be up to 50 different malt and grain whiskies in a blend. Brands like Johnnie Walker, Usher's, Bell's, Chivas Regal and Famous Grouse are good examples.

OTHER TYPES OF WHISKY

IRISH WHISKEY — There are two main types of Irish whiskey, although you might find them harder to locate than Scotch whiskies. Considering the fact that whisky owes its origins to Gaelic culture, they have been left behind in the sales and marketing stakes. Irish whiskey differs in that peat is hardly ever used in the malting process, so the smoky, earthy overtones of Scotch malts are not present. One notable exception is Connemara Peated Irish Malt (double distilled) whiskey.

IRISH POT STILL WHISKEY — The main difference between Scotch malt and Irish malt is that most Irish malt is distilled three times instead of twice. It is made using both malted and unmalted barley, with the unmalted variety as the main component. Irish pot whiskey is found in many blends, but there are only two pot still whiskeys marketed on their own: Green Spot and Redbreast.

BLENDED IRISH WHISKEY — Pot still whiskey goes into making blended Irish whiskey, along with grain whiskey and sometimes single malt, as well.

AMERICAN WHISKEYS

BOURBON — Bourbon is American whiskey made from grain, yeast and water. At least 51% of the grain must be maize. Other cereals used are malted and unmalted barley, wheat and rye. Bourbon is fermented with yeast and distilled in column stills on a continuous basis, unlike the batched malt whisky produced in Scotland. It must be stored in oak casks to mature for at least two years. Bourbon gets its name from Bourbon County, in Kentucky, but it can be distilled anywhere in the US. An example you may have heard of is Jim Beam Black bourbon whiskey.

TENNESSEE WHISKEY — Tennessee whiskey is made in the same way as bourbon, but has an extra process in its making. This is called the Lincoln County Process and involves filtering the new spirit through maple charcoal before maturing it in a barrel. This not only filters out impurities but is said to produce a smoother whiskey. I'll take my son's word for it. Jack Daniel's is a famous example.

RYE WHISKEY — Although most US whiskeys are dominated by maize, this is the exception. At least 51% of the grain must be rye, although the proportion is often considerably more. This drink had apparently become less popular and was a rarity, although it seems to be on the increase again. The name Rittenhouse — as in Rittenhouse Rye — is unknown to me, except in the context of the Marx Brothers, when Groucho, on being introduced to his hostess, Mrs Rittenhouse, wryly retorted: 'You've got a rotten house, Mrs Rittenhouse'. I can't comment on the Rittenhouse Rye, but I am informed that it is oily and unremarkable.

OTHER WORLD WHISKIES

CANADIAN WHISKY — Canadian whisky is often called rye, although I'm told that it is quite different from the American version. The only Canadian I know is teetotal, so she can't help me. This type of rye is a blend of several ryes mixed with other grain whisky. It may also contain just under 10% of something else to flavour it. This may be bourbon or even fruit juice. Well, I've heard of people putting orange in their whisky as a mixer, but not actually in the bottle. The whisky is aged in used oak barrels for a minimum of three years, with four to six years being the norm. Virtually all Canadian whiskies are blended from grain whiskies of different ages.

JAPANESE WHISKY — This type of whisky has been developed as a clone of Scotch whisky, although it has now taken on a character of its own. Malt whisky is double distilled in pot stills from lightly peated, malted barley. Standard Japanese whisky is a blend of malt whisky, which can be Japanese or Scotch in origin, and Japanese grain whisky.

INDIAN WHISKY — India produces a large amount of whisky made from various barley and non-barley ingredients. One of the most well known is Amrut Cask Strength.

A large number of other countries are producing their own brands of whisky nowadays, including Australia, Austria, Belgium, Brazil, Finland, France, Germany, Holland, New Zealand, Pakistan, South Africa, South Korea, Switzerland, Sweden, Thailand, Turkey, Uruguay, Venezuela and Wales. There's even whisky being made in Cornwall. You can find a list of some brands later in the book (see pages 114-127).

HOW IS SCOTCH WHISKY MADE?

HOW IS SCOTCH WHISKY MADE?

The actual business of distilling spirit for making whisky doesn't take too long: it's the process of maturing this spirit that takes time. Unlike vodka, which can be made, sold and consumed within a matter of days, whisky must be matured for at least three years. There are about 100 active distilleries in Scotland. The average production of each of them is between 1.2 million and 2 million litres (0.2 and 0.4 million gallons) a year. This means that the minimum amount of whisky stored in Scotland is 450,000,000 litres (or just under 100 million gallons), and this figure doesn't take into account the huge amount of whisky which is ageing for 10 to 30 years.

MALTING

Malt is made from barley or another grain, which has been steeped, germinated and dried for brewing, distilling or making vinegar. Malting happens when grain becomes damp and starts to germinate. It would have happened by accident originally and then been refined over the years.

Nowadays, the whole malting process is carefully controlled. If germination isn't successful, then the chemical process, which begins here, won't happen. The grain must be fully ripe and dry before processing. If the grain is too wet it will go mouldy. It must be high in starch and low in protein and nitrogen. This means that there must not have been too much fertiliser added to the soil.

Barley is kept dry in huge silos until required. This ensures that when the malting process begins the grain is in prime condition. Malting begins with steeping, which is a bit like being thrown out from

FLOW CHART OF WHISKY DISTILLERY PROCESS

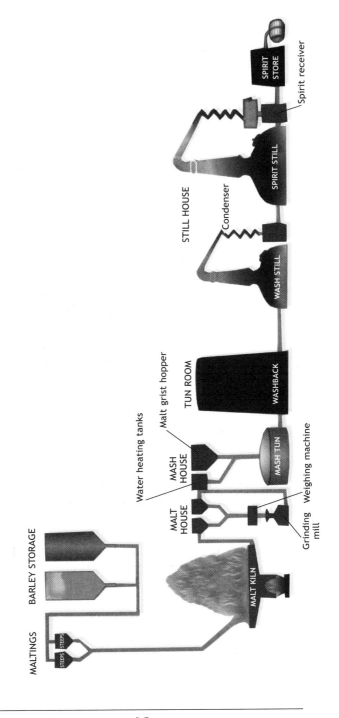

under a light, warm duvet and being tipped into a cold bath or shower. The grain swells in size as it absorbs the water, and an enzyme is activated which breaks down cell walls to reach the energy of the grains in the form of starch. At this stage, if left to its own devices, the grain would germinate and start to grow by sprouting and putting out tiny roots, using the starch released. This would mean that there would be less starch contained in the grain. The starches released during germination become sugars, which, in turn, make alcohol, so the process has to be stopped. After all, the best grain should give the best yields.

Today, most of the malting is carried out by a few specialists, who supply malt to the distilleries. A few, such as Bowmore, Highland Park and Laphroaig, still malt some of their own barley, but all rely on the specialists for at least half of their malt. Industrial malters now use automated systems with huge rotating drums and kilns, to dry the grain. Originally, peat would have provided the fuel, but nowadays other fuels are used, with the addition of peat smoke offering flavour and aroma. Smoke from peat fires in the kiln determines the taste of many whiskies, and the level of peat can be controlled.

MASHING

Dried malt — or other grain — is ground into a very coarse sort of flour, called *grist*. This process takes place in a mill hopper, which is a bit like an enormous coffee grinder. Two rollers inside crack the husk and pummel the grain. It is then tipped into the *mash tun*, rather like an enormous percolator. Hot water extracts all the goodness, namely soluble sugars, from the grist. Around one part grist to four parts water starts to make a porridge. The liquid is heated to around 64°C (147°F), which is the highest temperature the grist can take without destroying the enzymes. Enzymes get to work to break down the sugars (maltose). Rakes inside the mash tun stir up the syrupy mix, called a *wort*. After about 30 minutes the plates on the bottom of the mash tun, which have holes in them, are opened. The wort drains out, leaving the porridge-like grist behind. This still has plenty of goodies left in it, so it goes back through hotter water for two more extractions. The last one, *spargeing*, reaches 85°C (185°F) and takes about 15 minutes. This liquid becomes the first water for the next mashing. The solids left behind (*draff*) are mixed with residue from a later process and turned into a rich, protein-filled cattle feed. Lucky cattle!

FERMENTATION

The wort is transferred to a large vessel, called a *washback*, until it is about two thirds full. There may be several circular washbacks in any distillery. They measure about 3.7 meters (12 feet) in diameter and each holds thousands of litres of what will become a sort of beer. Fresh yeast is tipped onto the washback and the lid is closed. Living organisms like yeast need oxygen, so, in its absence, they start to feed on the sugars in the wort. This creates carbon dioxide, which sits on the top of the wash like a blanket.

HUBBLE BUBBLE

After a couple of hours something begins to erupt. The energy released is due to the chemical reaction taking place between the yeast and the sugar, resulting in an alcohol volume of about 5–7%. Imagine all that power unleashed! The washback has to be securely bolted to the floor, otherwise there might be a lot of rocking and rolling going on, and I don't mean of the musical variety. The staves of wooden washbacks, made from pine or larch, can be heard to groan under the strain. Metal rods, known as switchers, beat down the froth to avoid wash spilling all over the floor. In the past, young boys were given the job of switching, using brooms made from heather.

Fermentation takes just under two days, during which the temperature of the wash rises from 20°C (68°F) to 35°C (95°F). The last part of this process is a sort of secondary fermentation, carried out by bacteria, as the yeast cells are all exhausted after their day and night on the tiles — or, at least, in the wash. This is the difference between making whisky and beer. If allowed to continue, the non-sterile conditions would result in a very sour brew, ending as vinegar. At this point, I'm told that the wash is drinkable, but I think I'll pass on that one. It apparently has quite an effect on the bladder, which I certainly don't need!

Modern washbacks are sometimes made from steel instead of wood, for the convenience of cleaning. Too much bacteria can harm the yeast action, although wood does help to insulate the wash and keep the yeast happy.

DISTILLATION OF MALT WHISKY
Distillation is the process used to separate alcohol from water and other substances contained in the wash. This process, discovered hundred of years ago, is also used in the perfume industry. The principle is simple: water evaporates at 100°C (212°F) while alcohol does so from 80°C (176°F). Alcohol will therefore be transformed into vapour and rise in the still before the water begins evaporating.

Distillation increases the alcohol content and removes impurities. The still room is the heart of the distillery. The process has changed very little over the years, although the size of the pot stills and the level of technology have altered quite a lot. Basically, the still converts strong beer (the wash) into malt whisky. This is achieved by heating the wash to the point where it vaporises. The wash contains both 'good' and 'bad' alcohols, which have different boiling points. The job of the stillman — or the computer — is to collect the 'good' vapours for keeping while discarding the 'bad' vapours. Turning beer into whisky involves two processes, so every distillery producing malt whisky has two stills: a wash still and a spirit still.

Phase one: the wash still

A still is like a huge copper kettle. Wash is pumped into the first still until it is about two thirds full, then the heat is turned up. Since Victorian times, most distilleries have used a coil of copper inserted in the still, through which steam passes into the still, and this also helps to control the heat. Before this a fire was lit underneath the still. Some distilleries, like Glenfiddich, continue to use gas fires underneath the stills.

After about 30 minutes of boiling the heat is turned down. Alcohol boils at a lower rate than water. The vapours travel up to the top of the still. Modern stills have a pair of portholes for the stillman to view what is going on. These sight glasses enable the stillman to keep an eye on the still until only 'pot ale' remains. This is siphoned off and reduced to a syrup, to be used in cattle feed, as described earlier.

The condenser collects the vapours and returns them through a *lyne arm* to 'low wines', which are now at around 21% abv. This is where the second part of the process begins, because this percentage of alcohol is not enough to separate out the good and bad alcohols and is not yet strong enough to make whisky.

Phase two: the spirit still

The low wines are mixed with the residue of a second distillation, thereby raising the alcoholic volume to 28%. It is then pumped back for a further distillation. The spirit still is generally smaller than the first still, as there is less liquid to deal with.

At 90°C (194°F) the vapours rise and the foreshots climb up the neck of the still. The stillman looks at the spirit safe, which is a small glass and brass padlocked box. The *foreshots* condense back into a highly alcoholic liquid, which contains some pretty pungent impurities at first, including methanol. The strength gradually reduces as spirit flows back to the low wines and *feints receiver*.

Now is the time for the skilled stillman to judge when the foreshots are more or less gone and any remaining 'impurities' might be worth retaining. He conducts a test to look for the *middle cut*. This is done by mixing a little of the alcohol in the spirit safe with water. If the mix is cloudy, the foreshots haven't yet finished, but if it is clear, this is the signal for the middle cut to begin. A hydrometer can also be used to check the level of alcohol. The middle cut begins at about 75% abv and will keep going as the strength decreases and the feints begin. This third lot of spirit smells quite sweet and still has a high alcoholic content. As the feints continue to flow, the sweet smell becomes sweaty and a bit 'off'. The stillman has to judge when to direct the feints into the storage tank with the foreshots. This critical moment varies from one distillery to another, depending on the type of whisky each is aiming to produce, and can vary between 69% and 60% alcoholic content. In some modern distilleries the whole process is automatically timed; thanks to many lifetimes of experience, testing doesn't need to be carried out to the same degree.

THE SHAPE OF STILLS TO COME
There are numerous shapes and styles of pot still around today, and it is claimed that every single one is the result of a prolonged testing by trial and error. Some are onion shaped, with tapering tops, whereas others are short and squat. New stills are always copied from their predecessors at the distillery and they are

always made from copper. The shape and capacity of the new still needs to be the same as old ones, so that the quality of the whisky can be guaranteed.

WHY COPPER?
Copper is used because of the way it reacts with the spirit and helps to clear out sulphurous compounds, which would make the whisky undrinkable. If fact, many claim that, had copper not been used for the first stills, there might not be any whisky available to drink today.

As the vapours rise up the still, they condense against the copper walls and trickle back down into the pot. This is called reflux and increases in proportion to the height of the still and the angle of the lyne arm. If there is too much reflux, the whisky will be very clean and have little character, but if there is not enough, your hangover will tell you.

GRAIN WHISKY DISTILLATION
Most grain distilleries are found in the Lowlands of Scotland. They use Coffey stills, which have a different shape and run continuously, thereby operating on a much larger scale than malt distilleries. These column-shaped stills also produce whisky more cheaply. The grains used are usually maize, unmalted barley and wheat, along with some malted barley. These stills mean that the grain whisky matures more quickly and is less open to variable factors.

HANGOVER, ANYONE?
As a point of interest, when gin is distilled there are probably only about three additives or congeners, like juniper for example. Malt whisky and red wines can have up to 400 traces. I wondered why gin drinkers didn't get such awful hangovers as whisky drinkers, so there you are. I'm not giving up red wine though!

MATURING THE MALT WHISKY

After the distilling there's still a long way to go before the spirit can be called whisky. Since 1915, there has been a law in place, which states that maturing spirit must spend at least three years confined in oak casks before it can be classified or sold as whisky. It doesn't matter whether we are talking about single malt or grain whisky, the 'solitary confinement' rule is the same. So, as with good-quality red wine, there's no quick return on investment here. With wine you can, of course, drink it earlier, if desperate, but waiting a few years yields bigger dividends. Gin and vodka offer faster returns, in that they can be drunk immediately. Three years is only the minimum time, however, and many brands are matured for eight, ten or twelve years.

ROLL OUT THE BARRELS

Oak casks are essential for the whisky to mature, because they allow the spirit to breathe in air through pores in the wood and to give out alcoholic fumes through evaporation. This is called the 'Angel's share'.

Oak is the perfect wood for keeping liquids in, as it is tough and waterproof but pliable. I know this from experience, as the oak beams in our French house were once the masts of ships sailing up and down the Gironde estuary. Since then, they have supported our house for over 150 years, withstood a hurricane and were the only bits of wood not eaten by termites when we bought the place nearly 10 years ago. There were oak barrels in the cellar, too. The wood was okay, but the metal bands had rusted and fell to pieces when picked up. So oak is just too tough, even for termites!

RECYCLING CASKS

The casks must have been used already before being used to mature whisky, because new oak would have too much influence on the taste of the spirit. Here's a lucky bit of recycling, then. Keeping whisky in oak barrels changes the character and colour of the spirit. After distillation the whisky has little colour, but after a tidy stay in a barrel that once played host to Spanish sherry or American bourbon, the familiar golden tint is present. The type of cask chosen for maturing the whisky has a much bigger effect on the taste than the strain of barley used for distillation, and some experts would say that over two thirds of the flavour comes from maturation in the cask.

Sometimes, other barrels which have been used for port, Cognac, Madeira, Calvados, Chardonnay or Bordeaux wine are used. Some cynics put this down to fashion, and sometimes the whisky only enjoys a very limited stay in these barrels. They are said to give the whisky a wood finish. The Bordeaux wine is interesting, because our local French wine producers insist that the oak barrels they use must be renewed every three years or so because the oak flavour given to the wine is too strong for most people after that. Barrels are, therefore, renewed fairy regularly.

Bourbon production in the US provides an inexhaustible supply of used barrels to Scotch whisky producers, to the tune of about half a million every year. These barrels are made from American white oak, or *Quercus alba*. Bourbon requires new barrels, to give it the characteristic vanilla, honey and caramel flavour which is its trademark. Today, about 90% of Scotch whisky barrels come from America. They are shipped over as staves and reassembled as hogsheads, which are 250-litre (54-gallon) capacity casks.

These 'refilled hoggies' can be used up to a further six times. The more often a barrel is used, the less flavour is left in the wood to impart to the whisky, so the barrel may become exhausted, poor thing. I know a nice resting place for it in my garden....

SHERRY OR BOURBON?
Spanish sherry casks from Jerez are imported as 500-litre (108-gallon) barrels. Being twice as big, they can be used more often. When these barrels, made from European oak, *Quercus robur*, have previously held Oloroso sherry, an extra dimension is added to the whisky.

These two main types of barrels are made in different ways. The American ones are charred over a furnace to blacken them on the inside, thus helping to release flavour into the bourbon. The Spanish ones are toasted, rather than charred, and then quickly soaked in water. Bourbon is twice as strong as sherry, and stronger alcohol seeps deeper into the wood. This means that it also sucks out more flavour from the wood.

CASK TRIVIA
- The shape of the casks relates to storage problems on ships in days gone by. Sherry was carried on Spanish galleons. The slender shape of the butts was the best for storing on these ships.

- In contrast, Portuguese Port was stored in a more bulbous cask, tailored to Portuguese merchant ships.

- Oak used for American bourbon barrels is at least 80 years old.

- Some distilleries have their own cooperages, like Balvenie or Bruichladdich, but most outsource this to specialised companies. The most famous of them is the Speyside Cooperage, situated halfway between the Glenfiddich distillery and the centre of Dufftown. This cooperage has about 300,000 casks in stock.

- There are about 20 million casks in Scotland.

The Scotch whisky industry mainly uses three kinds of casks:

NAME	APPROX CAPACITY IN LITRES	APPROX CAPACITY IN GALLONS
Barrel	190	36
Hogshead	250	54
Butt	500	108

As a matter of interest — or for the quiz fans — other cask sizes are as follows:

NAME	APPROX CAPACITY IN LITRES	APPROX CAPACITY IN GALLONS
Pin	20	4.5
Firkin	40	9
Kilderkin	72	16

THE ANGEL'S SHARE

One financial consolation for producers who have to wait for their whisky to mature is that they don't get taxed on the whisky that evaporates — the so-called 'Angel's share'. Between 0.5–2% per year of the volume and alcohol evaporates during maturation, so that's quite a lot of spirit that the taxman misses out on.

There's an interesting conundrum here, in that very old whiskies, aged 30 years or more, could, theoretically, lose their right to be called whisky. Assuming a whisky has about 70% abv when it leaves the spirit still, and loses about 1% abv (or more) by volume per year, a 30-year-old whisky could have an abv percentage of lower than 40%, which is the lowest limit of alcohol permitted for it to be called whisky.

STORAGE CONDITIONS

The location of the storage warehouse for the whisky
in barrels has an effect on the speed of maturity. For
example, a stone store with an earth floor will have a
slower rate of evaporation than a modern warehouse
with temperature and humidity controls, but the
alcoholic strength may also decline faster, resulting in
a spirit of less than 40% abv. Traditional vaults are
said to provide a mellow spirit with greater
provenance. Many whiskies along the west coast and
on the Hebrides are stored on the coast, allowing the
salty sea air to pass on a tang to the spirit. The
reality today is that most whiskies are matured in
large central warehouses in the Scottish Lowlands,
close to the bottling facilities, far from sea influence.

COLOUR

The colour of the whisky can give a clue as to the type
of cask used to age the whisky, although sometimes a
legal 'spirit caramel' colouring is also added. Whisky
from sherry casks is usually darker or more amber in
colour, while whisky aged in casks that previously held
bourbon is usually a golden-yellow or honey colour.
Some special malts have been finished in rum casks
after 27 years in bourbon barrels, to give it the colour
of extra virgin olive oil. I think I'd prefer whisky to
look less like olive oil, personally.

BLENDING

Now we come to the parting or joining of the ways,
which ever way you look at it. Single malts, now properly
aged, can be mixed with other single malts from the
same distillery. These may be a different batch of the
same age or a different age. This whisky has to be
diluted to a strength between 40—46% abv. Sometimes a
'Cask Strength' edition, which is not diluted and may
have an alcohol content of 50—60%, is released. A
'Single Cask' edition may also be offered, where a
single cask has not been vatted with another cask.

Blended Scotch whiskies require a mix of dozens of different malt whiskies to be combined with grain whisky, in order to create the desired blend. Thus, for a malt whisky distillery, the single malt may get all of the glory, but the blends, ultimately, pay the bills.

Malt whisky and blended whisky are close cousins. About 95% of Scotch drunk is a blend of about a quarter to a third malt whisky mixed with grain whisky. The individual percentages of each malt whisky may be small, but each malt contributes its unique character to a blend. Very few distilleries could survive by selling only single malt. A few key players control the industry, selling both malt and grain whisky.

Blending whisky is a very complex operation — just like creating a new perfume. With so many variables affecting the casked whisky as it matures, there are infinite possibilities. Add to that the different ages, the proportions of this and that which can be included (maybe two or three grain whiskies and up to 30 or 40 malts), and you begin to see the choices. I see it as the same dilemma I have when spinning fleece and tops in different colours and textures. You don't always get what you want straight away, and some components — like yarn — which, on their own, are rich and beautiful, become lost in the overall mass of too much background colour. For example, if you want to make a blend with a Speyside heathery malt and then use an Islay with a fishy or smoked, peaty smell, you might not get what you bargained for.

Blending rooms tend to be secretive areas that are not open to public scrutiny, which is fair enough. Rather like libraries, but with bottles replacing books, the shelves will be full of small bottles containing variously coloured amber, golden and straw spirits. Once whisky is bottled it hardly alters, so each bottle will represent a sample from a distillery with the date of distillation, the type of cask used and where it was matured. Most of the work of blenders these days relates to checking and balancing, to ensure a consistency in the finished product and to avoid the odd cask which is different from its room-mates, and which might ruin a whole consignment. A blender will need to buy or produce a large number of different malt whiskies, in order to maintain the consistency of a blend. It is obviously impossible for a producer to have samples from every cask, when there may be millions of them maturing in a warehouse, but experienced blenders can 'nose' their way through dozens of samples in tulip-shaped glasses every day.

The modern industrial blender is a computerised version of an old-style paint blender from a DIY store. Pre-set quantities of whisky are taken from barrels, which roll along tracks over a narrow trough in the floor. The blending vat may contain up to 113,600 litres (25,000 gallons) of whisky. Sometimes, grain and malt whiskies are vatted separately before they are mixed together.

CHILL FILTRATION
Just before bottling, most of the whisky is chilled and filtered. The whisky is chilled to nearly freezing point (0°C, 32°F) and passed through a filter. This removes oils produced during distillation or extracted from the wooden casks. It also prevents the whisky from becoming cloudy when water or ice is added. The downside is that some would say that chill filtering also removes fragrance and flavour, so some single malts are not chilled.

BOTTLING
Whisky doesn't mature any more after bottling, so a 12-year-old whisky stays the same age, even 12 years later. Another interesting observation is that if a

blended bottle is labelled as 12-year-old whisky, this means that the youngest whisky in the blend has been matured in cask for at least 12 years before bottling, but there might well be some older whiskies present, as well. During bottling, the alcohol percentage needs to be reduced. This is the other time when the quality of water has an influence on the taste of the whisky. The minimum percentage of alcohol for whisky is 40%. Excise duty is calculated on the abv. As tax rates are high on spirits in the UK, the percentage is kept at 40%, although in other countries, where duty is lower, whiskies at 43% are more common.

Most distilleries, with few exceptions, don't bottle their own whiskies. This is done at specialised plants, although the responsibility for the bottling stays with the distillery. The suburbs of Edinburgh have several bottling plants belonging to distilleries or independent bottlers. These independent bottlers buy casks of whisky from one or several distilleries and mature them in their own warehouses or at the distillery. When ready for bottling, the whiskies are marketed under the name of the bottler, rather than the distillery.

A SHORT HISTORY OF SCOTCH WHISKY

HOW DID SCOTCH WHISKY ORIGINATE?

'To Friar John Cor, by order of the King, to make aqua vitae VIII bolls of malt.'
EXCHEQUER ROLLS 1494—1495

As with many products and brews which have developed from ancient times, the origins of whisky are open to debate. The date of the first-recorded distillation in Scotland came in 1494, when a Benedictine monk called John Cor was sold malt and allowed to distil it to make something called *aqua vitae*. This is Latin for 'water of life', which, in Gaelic was known as *uisge beatha*, pronounced rather like 'oosh-ki-ba'. Over the years this was shortened to 'uiskie' and later became whisky. But we've jumped ahead a few centuries, so let's go back and study some of the theories about how whisky first came to Scotland.

WHEN DID DISTILLING BEGIN?

Alcohol is produced naturally as a result of wild yeasts blowing in the wind and alighting on fruit, grapes or grains. Man has been making beer and wine for thousands of years, but to distil this into spirit took a bit more know-how. The exact time the first spirit was distilled is unknown, although in India they were making Arrack in 800 BC and the Chinese were probably producing spirit from rice even before then. In around 400 BC, Aristotle was studying weather and working out how the water cycle worked. He created a method of distilling seawater in a pan by boiling it and suspending balls of wool, to represent clouds, over it, to catch the vapours. He managed to show how seawater could be made drinkable and how liquids can be separated into various parts by distillation. The water evaporated, leaving the salt. This takes me back to primary school science lessons. Maybe we could add distillation, to brighten up the old experiments with salt and water! Whisky and other spirits have a lower boiling point than water, so vapour forms faster. The only problem is catching it.

The Ancient Egyptians already knew about distillation, but they were more interested in making perfume by this method. As a matter of interest, alcohol is said to come from the Arabic *al kuhl*, although how we get to a spirit from kohl, I can't quite see. Kohl was a lead compound used for eye make up, ground and applied to the lids to prevent sun damage.

The word spirit to define distilled alcohol is interesting, if not unsurprising, given the nature in which vapours rise. Religious teachings suggesting that the human spirit rises from the body after death may have something to do with this. In 1500, Hieronymous Braunschweig defined distillation as:

> *puryfyeng of the grosse from the fsbtyll and subtyll from the grosse*

So, there we have it! The nature of *aqua vitae* had been an obsession for hundreds of years. Men were studying the effects of alcohol on the body and using the rejuvenating and stimulating effects it could have on soldiers before and during battle. Certainly, monks and missionaries were aware of the medicinal qualities of spirit on healing wounds and dulling pain — and how many monasteries were responsible for the production of spirits and liqueurs, such as Benedictine?

THERE ARE THEORIES IN THE HILLSIDES

How did the monks in Scotland know how to distil? This is beginning to sound like a game of *Call My Bluff*. One theory is that whisky making developed from the ancient Celts, who brewed a sort of weak beer, made from malted barley and flavoured with heather. Archaeologists have found evidence to suggest that such brewing took place from at least 2000 BC.

This beer, low in alcohol, later became popular when barley needed to be used up, after a particularly wet harvest, when fermentation of the barley occurred. I'm not so convinced by this one, however, even though the ancients did make beer from cereals in a similar way to the first stages of making whisky. I think they needed divine intervention in the worldly guise of monks.

Another theory has it that the skills and know-how were brought from Ireland by missionary monks, who travelled to Scotland in the 4th and 5th centuries, spreading Christianity to the Picts in Scotland. These monks brought with them the first primitive stills, which they had learned of during visits to mainland Europe. The Picts found that they could create a stable alcoholic beverage by distilling their ale. Whisky distilling is said to have arrived in Kintyre and Islay, the closest onland points to Ireland. A third theory suggests that soldiers returning home from the Crusades, some time between the 11th and 13th centuries, brought back the techniques from the Arabs, who were among the first to understand distillation. There may even have been visits in the 9th century.

After the Norman invasion of Ireland in 1169, by Henry II, the troops are said to have been fond of a drop of *uisge beatha*. So, whatever the origin, it appears that by the 12th century both Ireland and Scotland were producing grain spirit. An ancient copper 'worm', used to condense spirit, was found in an Irish peat bog. Although, originally, it was thought to be a lot older, it was eventually dated to around 1400.

TUDOR TIMES
The whisky produced by Friar John Cor, in Fife, in 1494, from 'eight bolls of malt', would have been enough to produce about 1,500 bottles of whisky,

suggesting that distilling was already a well-established practice, and not solely for medicinal purposes. By 1503, Edinburgh's Guild of Surgeon Barbers was granted the right to make *aqua vitae*, and this right survived for 250 years.

The primitive equipment used back then, combined with the lack of scientific expertise, means the spirit produced in those days was probably extremely potent, and often even harmful. To be frank, the spirit would probably have left your throat feeling as if you had sandpapered it and then swallowed something scalding, while, simultaneously, someone was smacking you in the face! However, with improvements in methods and a sharing of expertise, considerable advances were made over the next couple of hundred years. It was found that running a pipe or worm, sticking out from a still, through cold water produced a lot more whisky than relying on cold air to cool it. During the mid 15th century, someone discovered that if you coiled the worm like a corkscrew you could condense even more of the alcoholic vapour. Still shapes changed about this time as well, to the now familiar squashed-pear shape. Some of this expertise undoubtedly came from the monks who were driven from their cloisters by Henry VIII, following the dissolution of the monasteries. Between 1539 and 1550, they probably had no other choice but to put their skills to use in a practical way.

Whisky first appears in historical records, when Tudor kings and queens began to consolidate English rule in Ireland. Queen Elizabeth I is said to have been fond of whisky, and had casks shipped to London on a regular basis. Suddenly, barley was in great demand, not only for bread and flour, but also for making whisky. A poor harvest prompted Mary, Queen of Scots to try to restrict the use of barley in 1555. An Act of Parliament in 1579 banned whisky making for a year, after another bad harvest, unless of course you were a member of the aristocracy, when it was still allowed. Queen Elizabeth I of England, however, declared that the people should have as much as they liked 'to warm their chilled stomachs'.

GUT ROT
The first whisky would have been made from whatever cereal was available. This pretty mean brew would have been drunk straight from the still, sometimes tempered with sugar, spices or herbs. Today's whisky-distilling process gets rid of many of the impurities or congeners (which can give you a terrible hangover) without removing all of them, which give it 'character'. It's a wonder that anyone knew who they were by the end of a session on the hard stuff, let alone being able to function in any capacity. Imagine the characters roaming the Highlands on a dark night!

JOINT GREASE
It must have had some good effects though, otherwise why would you risk making yourself feel worse? Whisky was used to rub onto aching joints, for cleaning wounds or probably for relieving pain by knocking the patient into oblivion. Whisky was also praised for the preservation of health, helping people to live a long life and for the relief of colic, palsy and even smallpox.

In his *Chronicles of England, Scotland and Ireland*, published in 1577, Raphael Holinshed describes the virtues of Uisge Beatha:

Being moderately taken,
it slows the age,
it cuts phlegm,
it lightens the mind,
it quickens the spirit,

> *it cures the dropsy,*
> *it heals the strangulation,*
> *it pounces the stone,*
> *its repels gravel,*
> *it pulls away ventositie,*
> *it kepyth and preserveth the head from whirling,*
> *the eyes from dazeyling,*
> *the tongue from lispying,*
> *the mouth from snufflying,*
> *the teeth from chatterying,*
> *the throat from rattlying,*
> *the weasan from stieflying,*
> *the stomach from womblying,*
> *the harte from swellying,*
> *the belly from wincying,*
> *the guts from rumblying,*
> *the hands from shiverying,*
> *the sinews from shrinkying,*
> *the veins from crumplying,*
> *the bones from achying,*
> *the marrow from soakying,*
> *and truly it is a sovereign liquor*
> *if it be orderly taken.*

PRETTY COMPREHENSIVE STUFF!

Whisky know-how spread to other parts of Scotland, supplying homes as a seasonal cottage industry. After harvesting had finished and the winter months had set in, any spare grain would be used by farmers to make whisky. Whisky was made on a small scale, usually on or near a farm and close to a water source, such as a mountain spring or burn. The spirit was double distilled and didn't get to age before being consumed at great strength. If there was a surplus, this whisky could be sold or bartered with. Every Highlander believed he had a right to distil his own requirements.

The first mention of *uisge* in Scottish annals came in the account of the funeral wake of a Highland chieftain, around 1618. The first taxes on whisky production were imposed in 1644, by the Scottish

Covenanting Parliament. The Malt Tax was supposed to raise money to pay for the Duke of Montrose's Highland army to fight for Charles I, but it was unpopular and almost impossible to collect. Nevertheless, the tax remained in place, despite widespread protests, until 1707. All this did was to make people more careful where they hid their stills. In 1682, a Board of Excise had been established for Ireland, with a separate board for England and Wales being established the following year. Scotland had to wait until the Act of Union of 1707, during which time malt taxes increased a lot.

FERINTOSH
The first distillery registered in Scotland was the Ferintosh distillery, owned by Duncan Forbes of Culloden and opened in the 1670s. It was sited on the Black Isle, near Inverness. Forbes was a prominent supporter of William of Orange, which is why the Jacobites burned it to the ground in 1689. As compensation, the Scottish Parliament allowed him to distil, free of duty, on his estate. This amounted to £40,000 per annum, an astonishing sum at the time. Mr Forbes and his family naturally became very rich. They were bought out for £21,580 in 1784, when the Wash Act ended the duty-free status, but three more distilleries were built on the same site. Ferintosh was, apparently, a cut above the 'hooch' being produced elsewhere. During its 100 years of production, it supplied two out of every three legal drinks of whisky, but, by 1780, there are said to have been about eight legal distilleries and 400 illegal ones.

The Scottish bard Robert Burns, a heavy drinker who was very partial to many a wee dram of whisky, briefly became an excise man himself. It must have been like letting a fox guard the chickens. He lamented the passing of Ferintosh:

O thou, my Muse! guid, auld Scotch Drink!
Whether thro' wimplin worms thou jink,
Or, richly brown, ream owre the brink,
In glorious faem,
Inspire me, till I lisp an' wink,
To sing thy name!

O Whisky! soul o' plays an' pranks!
Accept a Bardie's gratefu' thanks!
When wanting thee, what tuneless cranks
Are my poor Verses!
Thou comes — they rattle i' their ranks
At ither's arses!

Thee, Ferintosh! O sadly lost!
Scotland's lament frae coast to coast!
Now colic grips, an' barkin hoast
May kill us a';
For loyal Forbes' chartered boast
Is taen awa!

Extracts from *Scotch Drink* by Robert Burns, 1785

The 18th century saw turbulent times in Scotland, with a fair amount of opposition to the Act of Union, following the English Civil War. Many wanted a Stuart king to be restored to the throne. The Jacobite rebellion of 1745 finally ended with the Battle of Culloden, in 1746. The malt taxes hit beer as well as whisky and riots spread across the country. The most serious of these had happened in June 1725, when revenue men arrived at the Maltsters and were met by a large crowd. Troops were called and shots were fired, resulting in the deaths of eight civilians.

Imagine excise men having to impose English laws on Scottish Highlanders with illicit whisky stills: not an encouraging prospect, really. The Scottish Excise Board in Edinburgh was run by English officers. These officers, called gaugers, could do little in the face of organised dissent. Smuggling and illicit whisky making were seen as a natural way of restoring the balance and undermining the English imposition of a tax on their national drink. Finally, the malt duty was reduced to half the English rate.

The Act of Union made tax on whisky one of the main sources of revenue in Scotland. Interestingly, the English government reduced the tax on English gin at the same time. Obviously, however, not everyone admitted to keeping and running stills in the remote Highlands of Scotland. By the end of the 18th century, smuggling the hooch to avoid paying duty was big business, and nobody was fooled as to the number of illicit stills tucked away in the remote crags and bothies of the Highlands and Islands. Illegal stills were cleverly concealed in nooks and crannies in the hills. One group channelled the smoke from the peat fire underground for 70 yards (64 metres) to a cottage, where it could be sent up the chimney. All levels of society seemed to be tolerant of the clandestine nature of distilling. On Orkney, the story goes that a vicar used a funeral service to cover up the presence of whisky casks hidden in the church.

The 1784 Wash Act, which followed a particularly bad harvest and widespread famine, granted anyone north of the Highland Line exemption from malt tax, if the spirit was produced and consumed within the same parish. This was great for the Highlanders, but deeply resented by the Lowlanders. The problem of illicit distillation and smuggling seems to have been widespread. Around 1794, a vicar from Islay wrote:

> This island hath the liberty of brewing whisky, without being under the necessity of paying the vital Excise Duty to the government. We have not an Excise Officer on the whole island. The quantity therefore of whisky made here is great, and the evil that follows drinking to excess of this liquor is very visible on this island.

Some say that Islay was exempt from paying excise to the Crown, but, in fact, it seems that the island paid 'In Farm' duties to the laird of the island instead. Whether the laird passed on these taxes isn't clear, but excise men certainly didn't want to travel to the island where there were 'wild barbarous people'. This would account for the large number of distilleries that sprang up on the island and their location there today. An alternative theory is that Islay was physically too wild, hostile and remote to allow a customs officer to be stationed there permanently.

Over the 150 years of smuggling and illicit distillation, there doesn't seem to have been any moral dilemma or stigma involved. It was a 'them and us' situation, with the English gaugers at a distinct disadvantage at first, regarding language and terrain. By the 1820s, as many as 14,000 illicit stills were being confiscated every year. Even so, more than half the whisky drunk in Scotland was consumed without contributing a penny in duty.

The government, however, was keen to take control and assert their authority by stamping out the illegal trade. They tried to crack down by banning wash stills of less than 1,818 litres (400 gallons) capacity and spirit stills of less than 455 litres (100 gallons), but the plan backfired, because small stills were hard to spot and higher tax on legal whisky made the illegal stuff taste even better. Perhaps it was because the smaller, Highland stills produced whisky at a slower pace than the legal ones further south. Even King George IV demanded some illicit Glenlivet from Speyside, when he landed in Edinburgh for a state visit in 1822.

Production of illicit whisky proliferated in the Highlands. Equipment was easily transportable and the smugglers or bootleggers could hide in innumerable glens. Look-outs were posted on nearby outcrops of rock to give notice of approaching excise men or gaugers. Gangs of up to 50 men could gather, and, by the end of the 18th century several parts of Scotland were considered no-go areas for excisemen, who would venture there reluctantly and at their own peril.

THE WORM THAT TURNED

The most valuable part of the still was the copper coil or worm. When immersed in a cask and cooled by the river's water, it aided the condensation of spirit vapours into a distilled liquor. The authorities had the brilliant idea of offering £5 to anyone who would 'grass' on the existence of an illicit still. The distillers, however, turned this situation around quite neatly to their own advantage. Whenever a worm wore out, the smuggler just needed to inform on the location of the still, where he had abandoned the old worm. The reward collected would allow the purchase of a brand new coil, without delay, and the setting up of the replacement still at a new site.

LOWLAND DISTILLERIES

The late 18th century saw a big boost to the Lowland distilleries, mainly owned by the Stein and Haig families, who, at one time, controlled half of the licensed production for the whole of Scotland. Robert Stein later invented a continuous still method, which he patented in 1827. One such plant, Kilbagie in Clackmannanshire, employed 300 people, but, by the mid 19th century, this had been converted to a manure factory. If the spirit produced was too poor in quality for the Scottish palate, and was:

> 'only fitted for the most vulgar and fireloving palates'

then the solution was to export it to England, where it could be turned into gin.

LEGALISATION

The smuggling situation prompted the Duke of Gordon to propose in the House of Lords that the government should make it profitable to produce whisky legally. Obviously, there was no conflict of interest: he just happened to own extensive acres, where some of the finest illicit whisky in Scotland was being produced. I'm sure he was a philanthropist at heart.

Finally, in 1823, an Excise Act was passed, which reduced taxes on Scotch whisky to a manageable level. Distillers making over 182 litres (40 gallons) per year could be licensed for £10. Those who made less were shut down. At this point, most of the larger distillers became legal taxpaying businesses. Those who declined to pay would be hunted out by English excise men and closed down. This Excise Act coincided with the beginnings of the Industrial Revolution, so this really started the whisky industry on a commercial basis, rather than as the cottage industry it had been before. Entrepreneurs could make good money out of it! At its height, there were 329 licensed distilleries. We can only guess how many illicit stills remained.

GAUGING SUCCESS

Marketing the whisky across Scotland presented some challenges when the gaugers were more efficient at their job, but there was always the old trick of sending out a decoy cask or two with a mule in one direction while the main consignment went the other way. The most notorious gauger was Malcolm Gillespie, who, in a long and successful career in the Aberdeen region, managed to impound over 6,500 barrels of whisky, along with over 400 stills and more than 150 horses. Unfortunately, this gamekeeper apparently turned poacher, and was hanged for corruption in 1827.

IRISH COFFEY

The next 'big thing' in whisky making was due to the discovery of an Irishman called Aeneas Coffey, who, by a strange twist, was employed as an excise man in Dublin. Robert Stein had developed a continuous distillation method in 1827, but, in 1831, Coffey invented the still that would revolutionise the industry, allowing whisky to be made in a continuous process that offered a great deal more of the spirit than the pot stills had allowed before. The method was more efficient and could be carried out on a larger scale, making cheaper whisky from other grains as well as barley.

The Coffey still had two columns separated by a set of perforated plates. The wash was heated up to near boiling point before being passed down the first column then pushed up the other column, where it met low-pressure steam. The spirit vaporised, allowing more volatile spirit vapours to rise, where they were condensed by the cold wash. It tasted dreadful and could only be made into gin. It's enough to put you off gin for life, isn't it? However, once cast iron was replaced by copper, things could only get better. Grain whisky began to be produced to fulfil needs across the world.

At this point, I can't leave out one of my favourite Victorian poets, William Topaz McGonnagall, 1825–1902. This extract is from his punchily titled *A New Temperance Poem, in Memory of my Departed Parents, who were Sober Living and God Fearing People*. That really is just the title! Along with words on porridge and national disasters, such as the Tay Bridge Disaster, he was a fierce opponent of alcohol in all forms.

> *My parents were sober living, and often did pray*
> *For their family to abstain from intoxicating*
> *   drink alway;*
> *Because they knew it would lead them astray*
> *Which no God fearing man will dare to gainsay.*

The Devil delights in leading the people astray,
So that he may fill his kingdom with them
*   without delay;*
It is the greatest pleasure he can really find,
To be the enemy of all mankind.

Luckily, McGonnagall and friends didn't get their way. Grain whisky was pronounced the 'Devil's drink' by the temperance movement and denounced as 'an apology for whisky' by traditionalists, who advocated sticking to 'the fruit of our own farmers, the manufacture of our friends and brethren'. Since legal production was no gauge to actual consumption, it isn't easy to say whether home consumption increased that much as a result of the Coffey still. In 1835, there were 230 distilleries, although this had dropped to 169, 10 years later. Once again, the railways helped to spread the word, and the grain whisky, southwards.

This gave rise to the boom in blended whisky. Coffey had apparently offered the invention to distillers in Ireland, but they declined, so he took the idea to Scotland. This was just another example of Ireland missing the boat where whisky or whiskey is concerned.

THE RAILWAYS

The Act of Union brought some prosperity to Scotland, but at a high price. Over the next 200 years, Glasgow became rich on tobacco, sugar and cotton trade, and the wealth went into mining, iron production, ship-building and the railways. Some of this wealth was also used to set up distilleries. The arrival of the railways in Scotland during the latter half of the 19th century, was a real boon to the distillation industry. The concentration of distilleries in Speyside is not only due to the quality of water, but to the arrival of the railway line from Edinburgh to Inverness, allowing the easy movement of barley, coal and whisky stocks.

Read more later, about how the Strathspey Line helped to develop distillation on Speyside.

BEETLE BENEFITS

Another helping hand in the distillation and popularity of Scottish whisky came from France, in the last quarter of the 19th century. By the 1880s, the Phylloxera beetle had devastated the vineyards of France. Wine, port and cognac began to disappear from cellars everywhere. Scottish entrepreneurs were quick to take advantage of this catastrophe and cash in with their new blends of whisky, which appealed to the southern palates of the English and other foreign consumers. By the time the French wine industry recovered, Scotch whisky had replaced cognac as the spirit of choice.

INTO THE BLENDER

The middle and upper classes who visited Scotland for grouse shooting or salmon fishing, found the malt whiskies of the Highlands robust and stimulating, but the taste just wasn't the same when transported south. They were too strong and spirited for home consumption, but that changed with the entrepreneurial spirit of a few Scots like the Walker family and Tommy Dewar. Johnnie Walker, a Kilmarnock grocer, was one of the first to produce a blend. Many grocers, such as the Chivas brothers in Aberdeen and Arthur Bell in Perth, realised the economic benefits of using cheaper, less flavoursome grain whisky added to malt whiskies to zap it up a bit.

The produce of the distilleries was shipped, in casks, to Glasgow and Edinburgh by either sea, cart or (later) rail. This early use of water transport accounts for the predominance of distilleries on the Scottish shorelines. It was the coming of the railways and the introduction of cheap glass bottle production which really kick-started the business and spread it further south. This was the halcyon era for Scotch.

Blenders would buy casks of malt and grain whisky and blend them in the cellars. They could then be sold in the shops in stone bottles or jars. Tommy Dewar was the son of a blender from Perth. In 1885, he started Dewars White label. By 1900, he had produced over 4,546,000 litres (1 million gallons) of the spirit. Other, now famous, names began production around the same time: James Buchanan made Black and White and Peter Mackie, White Horse. Famous Grouse originated in Perth, at the hands of Matthew Gloag, and Bell's was registered by Arthur Bell in 1896. Chivas Regal first became available in 1909.

LITTLE CHANGE IN METHODS

Few things have changed in the art of malt whisky distillation since the early days. The raw ingredients have remained the same, as has the shape of stills. Perhaps the only big change has been in the malting process. Traditionally, this was always done at the distillery. After being steeped in cold water, the barley was then spread out on the stone floor of a barn to dry and germinate. This malt had to be turned frequently with a wide wooden shovel to stop it sticking together in clumps. After about a week, the malted barley was laid over a wire mesh placed over a large kiln. The most common fuel in the Western Isles and the Highlands was peat, which was cut and dried during the spring months. There is no smell to peat until it is burnt, but smouldering point peat impregnates the malt it is drying with pungent blue smoke. Only a few distilleries, including Highland Park in Orkney, Balvenie and Laphroaig, still malt some of their own barley today, but nobody malts enough for their entire needs.

UN PETIT PROBLÈME

It is this aroma that is most commonly identified in the malts of the west coast — and, incidentally, what made our French neighbour think there was something wrong with the Bowmore we gave him some time ago. He is only used to drinking blends, bought in Spain for mixing with cola. He and some friends, after a couple of tries, thought that the peaty taste, characteristic of such fine malts, was a chemical which had interfered with the whisky, so he gladly gave back the major part of the bottle in exchange for a blended whisky instead! *Chacun à son goût*, as they say in France.

BOOM AND BUST

By the end of Queen Victoria's reign, whisky was in great demand and business was booming. Entrepreneurs and speculators were keen to invest in the trade by setting up new distilleries. A specialist architect, Charles Doig of Elgin, was busy designing distinctive pagoda-style roofs for many Speyside concerns. Banks were keen to lend money and investors were looking for a quick return. Does this sound familiar at all? Mergers, conversions of breweries and investment in bulk whisky could all reap rewards — or for a while at least.

The spectacular turn in fortunes came after R. and W. Pattison, blenders from Leith, became a public company in 1896. Shares were six times oversubscribed. Two years later, after spending £60,000 on advertising, the business was in trouble. The company collapsed and took 10 other firms with it. R. and W. (Robert and Walter) went to prison for fraud. They had, among other things, been selling whisky as 'malt' when it was in fact 99% grain. By the end of the century, whisky stocks had reached 409,148,100 litres (90 million gallons), worth around £15 million. The Pattisons' share of this was only £144,000, but the rot had set in and had left a deep impression on the Distillers Company Limited (DCL), founded in 1877.

DISTILLERS COMPANY

This was an amalgamation of grain distillers, which swallowed up struggling distilleries across the country. One thing that the Pattison scandal showed was that blending needed to be controlled. The very term whisky needed to be defined. Could it come from a continuous (patent) still as well as a pot still? The percentage of malt within blends needed to be considered, as there were huge variations of between 10% and 50% malt included.

Another problem was that the duty on blended Scotch was pushed up to two shillings and sixpence per bottle in the 1909 budget. Scandalous! This led to a fall in consumption, as planned by the government of Lloyd George, and a fall in excise of a million pounds. At the start of World War I, there were added calls for drunkenness to be curbed. It was decided that mature whisky was less harmful than the cheaper, young, fiery stuff floating about, so a law was passed in 1915, forcing the producers to mature the spirit for at least three years in casks.

During World War I, distilling was controlled and the authorities tried to reduce the strength of spirit sold, especially near munitions factories. William Ross, chairman of the DCL, led the move to rationalise the industry and prevent the rise and fall in demand, as well as keep out unscrupulous competition. A further blow came from the US, when Prohibition, officially, at least, closed off another market. This meant that, in 1927, there were only 84 distilleries instead of the 124 there had been only two years earlier. In fact, plenty of Scotch still found its way into the US during Prohibition during the 1920s.

Within five years, the number of distilleries had halved again, because of the Great Depression, and, in 1933, the only distilleries producing whisky were Glenlivet and Glen Grant. This was a deliberate attempt to save what was left of the industry until after the recession. Shipbuilding had been decimated and unemployment was terrible. One thousand jobs were threatened in the distillery industry and, with the market drying up in the US, things were extremely bleak.

When Franklin D. Roosevelt repealed Prohibition in America, however, and extra import duty was reduced, the shipments began again, so by 1939, the US was importing 21,821,232 litres (4.8 million gallons) of whisky. Once again, grain was short and production was restricted, but at least the prime minister, Winston Churchill, was a whisky devotee, when he couldn't get hold of brandy or Champagne. He said that on no account was barley grown for whisky to be reduced in quantity, being an invaluable export and dollar producer, which took years to mature. A man of forethought! Sales were pitched towards the US and a doubling of prices restricted the home sales. This time, many distilleries managed to stay open. Being in short supply at home and well known in America only helped to keep Scotch in the public eye.

After World War II, Britain needed to export to balance trade, so around a third — 27,276,540 litres (6 million gallons) — of all whisky produced was exported. Half of this went to the US. Once again, there was big under the counter trade, with one in three bottles drunk in Britain said to be bought on the black market. Once trade restrictions were lifted, optimism and expansion proceeded, with the 1950s seeing new stills and building work being undertaken. Since then, there has been a polarisation of distillery ownership into increasingly powerful drinks companies.

THE WHISKY REGIONS OF SCOTLAND

SCOTLAND'S GEOLOGY

Water for whisky making is best if it has passed over or through old rocks. The table below shows the geological succession of rocks. Young rocks usually lie over older ones, and a quick look at the geology of Scotland shows why some areas support distilleries.

ERA	GEOLOGICAL PERIOD	APPROX AGE IN MILLIONS OF YEARS
	Recent	0.01—0
Quaternary	Pleistocene	2
Tertiary	Pliocene	7
	Miocene	26
	Oligocene	38
	Eocene	54
	Palaeocene	65
Mesozoic	Cretaceous	136
	Jurassic	195
	Triassic	225
Palaeozoic	Permian	280
	Carboniferous	345
	Devonian	395
	Silurian	440
	Ordovician	500
	Cambrian	570
	Precambrian	
Origin of the Earth		4500

GEOLOGICAL TIMESCALE
Scotland is divided, geologically, into regions which correspond, more or less, to the four main whisky regions:

• Highlands
• Islands

- Lowlands
- Speyside (incorporated into the Highland region geologically)

Almost 3,000 million years of activity have contributed to the geology of Scotland as we know it. In that time, it has seen several climatic changes and the current landscape has undergone many topographical changes. What Scotland is now, has, in the past, been a desert, a tropical swamp, a volcanic landscape and an ocean floor, and it has endured countless ice ages.

THE HIGHLANDS (including Speyside)

The northern and west Highlands lie north of the Great Glen Fault, and have some of the most varied geology as well as the most spectacular scenery. This fault contains the famous Loch Ness and, at its north-eastern end, the Moray Firth. The rocks have been heated and compressed below the earth's surface, and are called metamorphic rocks. Over these, 1,000 million-year-old sandstones have been laid down by ancient rivers and these rocks now form mountains. Ordovician and Cambrian rocks, estimated at between 450 and 550 million years old, lie along the west coast. The Highlands continue below the Great Glen Fault and show a range of metamorphic rocks. South of the Moray Firth are areas of Permian and Triassic rock, which include fossils from 250 million years ago. The youngest rocks date from the Jurassic period. In this region is the important whisky producing area of Speyside, which supports over 40 distilleries today. The Orkney Islands are considered to be part of the Highland region.

LOWLANDS

The so-called Lowland region of Scotland is made up of the Midland Valley and the Southern Uplands. It reaches from Stirling and Perth in the north to the borders with England in the south. Much of the

Southern Uplands is made up of Ordovician and Silurian rocks, so we are still talking about very old rocks here, although the Lowland areas support fewer distilleries, widely spread across the region. What is left of 60 million-year-old volcanic activity is still in evidence, and the area contains a wide variety of glacial features, coastal landforms and active river systems. The whole area was changed by glacial erosion and deposition during the Ice Age, shaping and deepening valleys. The lower land is mostly covered by deposits of till, sand and gravel from the last ice age.

ISLANDS

The Islands of the Hebrides, Skye, Mull and Islay make up the final whisky region of Scotland, and also a separate geological region. The rocks around most of the Outer Hebrides, around Lewis, represent the oldest rocks seen in Britain, dating back about 3,000 million years. These were mostly granites, and have gone through more changes and upheavals than I care to mention.

On Skye and Rum there are layers of old red sandstones, which were laid down about 1,000 million years ago. Also on Skye, there are rocks laid down in a shallow sea between around 550 and 450 million years ago. There are also sedimentary rocks from the Triassic, Jurassic and Cretaceous eras. Add a touch of volcanic behaviour and you have a picture of a time when north-west Europe was being torn away from North America by the formation of the North Atlantic. Oh, and, just for good measure, we can add heavily ice-scoured mountains as well.

So what has this potted geology lesson got to do with the taste of whisky? Quite a lot, it seems. Research carried out by geologists has confirmed the suspicion that distilleries in areas where the rocks are distinctive and old can expect to produce whiskies of unusual character. For example, Bladnoch, in the Lowlands, is different from other distilleries because the water here rises from Silurian rock strata. Other distilleries are said to have a distinctive flavour because of carboniferous rocks south of the Firth of Forth. Highland malts, like Glenfiddich, are said to be fruity, whereas others in the area are more nutty or tinged with mustard. When plotted onto a geological map, they correspond to significant local distinctions. The oldest rocks are found on Islay, and the water taken for the distilleries at Bruichladdich and Bowmore, both known for their complex and somewhat unusual flavours, has the experience of passing over rocks which are 600 to 800 million years old.

It's not only the rocks and water that contribute to the taste of the whisky. The following may also have an effect:

• local vegetation
• choice of barley used
• the malting process
• peat used for drying malt
• yeast used in brewing
• material the fermenting vessel is made from
• shape of stills
• oak casks and previous contents
• maturation time
• position of warehouse used for maturation.

THE WHISKY REGIONS OF SCOTLAND

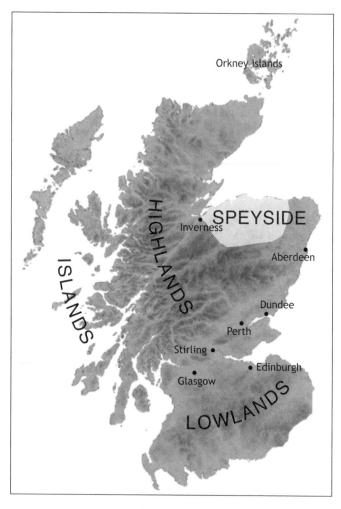

SPEYSIDE

The River Spey is a fast-moving river, flowing for over 100 miles from its source in the Cairngorms. This region is situated in north-east Scotland, around and between the towns of Grantown-on-Spey, Elgin, Dufftown and Keith, and has the greatest concentration of malt whisky distilleries in the world. There are several reasons for this, the first of which is related to rocks and water. Added to this, the remoteness of the area, availability of fuel, some local barley in an area of mainly subsistence farming and the fact that success breeds success, all colour the picture.

We know that quantities of good-quality, clean water are need to make whisky, but it is not only the River Spey which provides this commodity; underground springs are tapped by the distilleries, rather than removing water from the river.

The remoteness of the area had a lot to do with whisky making in the early days. Because of the taxes levied on whisky, there was, for at least 150 years, every incentive to make whisky on the quiet. A remote area like this was ideal, with many passes and routeways impassable for many months in wintertime: exactly when the distillation took place. The rugged terrain made life extremely hazardous for the intrepid excisemen, who dared to venture off the beaten track, in the hope of catching bootleggers and confiscating stills and whisky. Ask anyone who has tried to cross a mature heather moor in winter, with the rain and wind beating in your face and no track visible, let alone the visibility to find a needle in a haystack.

The peat moors formed by the build up of heather offered a readily available fuel for malting the barley and firing the stills. There had always been a tradition locally of brewing ale from heather, so part of the process was already established. By the time the industry was legalised in the 1820s, the expertise was well established, and this remained the case until the development of grain whisky distillation, after the Coffey still had been invented, when the remoteness of Speyside from the blending centres around Glasgow became more of a disadvantage.

The building of the railways was vital for the region, and, once this was accomplished, business once again boomed. In 1870, there were only 16 distilleries in Speyside, even though whisky was becoming big business. Further south, in Campbeltown, there were more well-established stills and transport was easier. In 1867, the Strathspey line opened, and the first distillery to be built alongside the railway was Cragganmore, built near Ballindalloch station, with its own sidings running into the distillery yard. The owner, John Smith, was a bit of a train enthusiast it seems, as well as a shrewd businessman. He loved to travel by train, even though his size meant that he couldn't get through the doors of the passenger carriages. Instead, he travelled in the guard's van. Other distilleries which grew up close to the Strathspey Line were Ballindalloch, Aberlour, Craigellachie and Knockando. Sadly, the line shut down in the 1960s, but part now forms the Speyside Way, a 96 km (60 mile) long walk way.

The Strathspey line had special sidings, delivering grain, fuel and casks to distilleries and taking casks of whisky away for blending. A total of 23 new distilleries opened during the 1880s and 1890s, thanks to the rail links, which also helped in the delivery of coal to the region, once the kilns previously fired with peat switched to coal as a fuel.

There are still over 40 distilleries working on Speyside today. The characteristic taste of most Speyside whiskies is a light peatiness with a touch of heather sweetness. There are, as always, a few notable exceptions. Blenders very much welcome the complex single malts produced in this region, although this means that a number of single malts are in danger of losing their personalities, as their output is used more and more to complement the blends required to suit modern tastes and wallets.

SPEYSIDE MALT DISTILLERIES

Every effort has been made to give up-to-date and relevant information in this section, but sometimes details change. It is best to check these first if you are planning a visit, or, indeed, to check whether they welcome visitors without booking. Numbers in brackets refer to the approximate location of the distilleries on the map of Speyside, below.

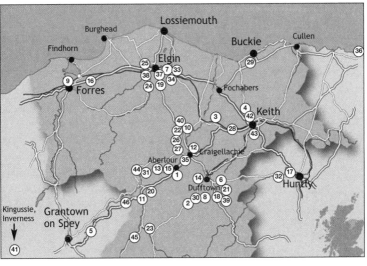

KEY TO MAP	(16) Glenburgie	(32) Knockdhu
(1) Aberlour	(17) Glendronach	(33) Linkwood
(2) Allt-a-Bhainne	(18) Glendullan	(34) Longmorn
(3) Auchroisk	(19) Glen Elgin	(35) Macallan
(4) Aultmore	(20) Glenfarclas	(36) Macduff
(5) Balmenach	(21) Glenfiddich	(37) Mannochmore
(6) Balvenie	(22) Glen Grant	(38) Miltonduff
(7) Ben Riach	(23) Glenlivet	(39) Mortlach
(8) Benrinnes	(24) Glenlossie	(40) Speyburn
(9) Benromach	(25) Glen Moray	(41) Speyside
(10) Cardhu	(26) Glenrothes	(42) Strathisla
(11) Cragganmore	(27) Glen Spey	(43) Strathmill
(12) Craigellachie	(28) Glentauchters	(44) Tamdhu
(13) Dailuaine	(29) Inchgower	(45) Tomintoul
(14) Dufftown	(30) Kininvie	(46) Tormore
(15) Glenallachie	(31) Knockando	

Aberlour (1)

Aberlour, Banffshire. Tel 01340 881249 www.aberlour.co.uk
The current distillery was rebuilt in the late 19th century.
Water came from the same well used by St Dunstan, but
now it comes from Ben Rinnes. Aberlour 10-year-old is said
to have a rich, honey taste with a hint of mint, and is
popular in France.

CAPACITY IN MILLION LITRES: 3

WHAT TO LOOK FOR: Aberlour 10-, 12- and 16-year-old Double
Cask Matured

Open to visitors

Allt-a-Bhainne (2)

Glenrinnes, Dufftown, Banffshire. Tel 01542 783200
www.pernod-ricard.com
Another modern distillery, opened in 1970, this one only
supplies malt for blends. Produces around 4 million litres
per year, mainly for Chivas Regal.

CAPACITY IN MILLION LITRES: 4

WHAT TO LOOK FOR: Light floral malt, only for blends

Auchroisk (3)

Ulben, Banffshire. Tel 01542 88500
www.malts.com
Built in 1974, most of what this distillery produces goes for
blending, although a 10-year-old malt is available. It is
popular in Spain as part of the J&B blend.

CAPACITY IN MILLION LITRES: 3

WHAT TO LOOK FOR: 10-year-old; 28-year-old rare malt

Open to visitors

Aultmore (4)

Keith, Banffshire. Tel 01542 881800
www.gordonandmacphail.com
Established in 1897, between the sea and Keith, this whisky
is now mostly used in blending. Only a small percentage is
bottled as Aultmore 12-year-old single malt.

CAPACITY IN MILLION LITRES: 1.8

WHAT TO LOOK FOR: Aultmore 12-year-old

Balmenach (5)
Cromdale, Grantown-on-Spey, Morayshire. Tel 01479 872569
www.balmenachdistillery.com
This distillery produces exclusively for blending. It was built
on the site of an illicit still which took a licence in 1824.
CAPACITY IN MILLION LITRES: 2
WHAT TO LOOK FOR: Blending only

Balvenie (6)
Dufftown, Banffshire. Tel 01340 820373
www.the balvenie.com
This is the partner distillery to Glenfiddich (see page 69).
Visitors can see original floor maltings and enjoy the smell
of malted barley. Its flavour has been described as toffee-
like, honeyed and rich fruit.
CAPACITY IN MILLION LITRES: 5.6
WHAT TO LOOK FOR: Doublewood 12-year-old; Founders Reserve
10-year-old; Single Barrel 15-year-old; Port Wood 21-year-old
Open to visitors

Ben Riach (7)
Longmorn, Elgin, Morayshire. 01343 862888
www.benriachdistilery.co.uk
Well-preserved floor maltings can be found on a visit here,
by appointment only. Founded in 1898, it was silent, after
three years, for another 65 years. It was then rebuilt in the
1960s, as a sister to Longmorn. The two malts are very
different, even though they share a water supply. Huge
varieties of rich, fruity, honeyed whiskies are produced.
CAPACITY IN MILLION LITRES: 2.5
WHAT TO LOOK FOR: Arumaticus, Authenticus, Authenticus
Fumosus; Ben Riach 15-year-old, in wood finishes;
Curiositas, Heart of Speyside 12-, 16- and 20-year-olds;
Hereditus Fumosus
Open to visitors

Benrinnes (8)
Aberlour, Banffshire. Tel 01340 872600 www.malts.com
One of 12 distilleries drawing water from springs percolating
through the granite of Ben Rinnes. Licensed in 1834, there are
six stills working in groups of three, providing a type of triple
distillation, mostly for blending.
CAPACITY IN MILLION LITRES: 2.6
WHAT TO LOOK FOR: Benrinnes 15-year-old

Benromach (9)

Forres, Morayshire. Tel 01309 675968 www.benromach.com
The smallest distillery on Speyside, this plant, owned by
independent bottlers, nevertheless, produces a range of
wood-finished whiskies and an organic variety. New stills were
installed when the plant reopened in 1998, 100 years after it
was founded.

CAPACITY IN MILLION LITRES: 0.5
WHAT TO LOOK FOR: Benromach 21- and 25-year-olds;
Benromach Organic; Benromach Peat Smoke; Benromach
Traditional; Portwood; Sassicaia; Tokaji
Open to visitors

Cardhu (10)

Aberlour, Banffshire. 01340 872555 www.malts.com
This distillery started as an illicit farm still, which became
licensed in 1824. It is one of the key malts used in Johnny
Walker blends, and is more popular as a single malt in Spain.
Cardhu 12-year-old is sweetish, with a clean taste. The
distillery was owned, until 1893, by the Cummings family,
who were innovators regarding workers' living conditions.
Elizabeth Cummings ran the business after being widowed
and became known as the 'Queen of the Whisky Trade'.

CAPACITY IN MILLION LITRES: 2.25
WHAT TO LOOK FOR: Cardhu 12-year-old
Open to visitors

Cragganmore (11)

Ballinddalloch, Banffshire. Tel 01807 500202
www.discoveringdistilleries.com
This distillery was built in 1869, ideally situated by the River
Spey for water power and spring water. Founded by John
Smith, a big (140-kg/22-stone) railway fan, it was the first
to be built by the railway, linking it to the blenders in the
south. A small distillery, set deeper into the Highlands than
other Speysides, it makes whisky with a sweet/sour fruit
flavour, unlike other local malts. Smith's odd-shaped stills
were copied in 1964 in order to double capacity.

CAPACITY IN MILLION LITRES: 1.5
WHAT TO LOOK FOR: Cragganmore 12-year-old; Cragganmore 17-
year-old (cask strength); Distiller's Edition Double Matured
Open to visitors

Craigellachie (12)
Craigellachie, Aberlour, Banffshire. Tel 01340 872971
www.dewars.com
Most of the output of this distillery is used for blends by
Dewar and Son, but a small amount is bottled. Founded in
1891 by a partnership of blenders, it was modernised in the
1960s.
CAPACITY IN MILLION LITRES: 2.25
WHAT TO LOOK FOR: Craigellachie 14-year-old

Dailuaine (13)
Aberlour, Banffshire. Tel 01340 872500 www.malts.com
Established in 1851, the ground was cleared to provide
railway sidings at the turn of the century for the delivery of
casks and barley by private train or puggy. Only a small
amount is sold as single malt. The rest goes to Johnny
Walker blends.
CAPACITY IN MILLION LITRES: 3
WHAT TO LOOK FOR: Dailuaine 16-year-old malt

Dufftown (14)
Dufftown, Keith, Banffshire. Tel 01340 822100
www.malts.com
Dufftown has a long fermentation period of about five days.
Founded in 1896, from a converted mill, most of the whisky
ends up in Bell's blends, with a small amount bottled.
CAPACITY IN MILLION LITRES: 4
WHAT TO LOOK FOR: Singleton of Dufftown, Flora and Fauna 15-
year-old

Glenallachie (15)
Aberlour, Banffshire. Tel 01340 871315
www.scotchwhisky.net
A modern distillery, founded in 1967 and designed by
William Delmé-Evans. Taken over by Pernod Ricard in 1989;
most goes for blending.
CAPACITY IN MILLION LITRES: 2.8
WHAT TO LOOK FOR: Cask strength 15-year-old

Glenburgie (16)
Forres, Morayshire. Tel 01343 850258 www.scotchwhisky.net
This distillery originated in 1829 and was expanded in the
1950s, to cope with the demand for blends. It was rebuilt in
2005. Most of the malt now goes for Ballantine's blends.
Rare bottlings of gingery, chocolaty characteristics sound
interesting.
CAPACITY IN MILLION LITRES: 4
WHAT TO LOOK FOR: Glenburgie 15-year-old

Glendronach (17)
Forgue, Huntley, Aberdeenshire. Tel 01466 730202
www.scotchwhisky.net
Reopened in 2002, to supply blends for Ballantine's, this is
sometimes classified as a Highland whisky, coming from the
extreme east of the Speyside region. It is a traditional
distillery, with wooden washbacks, floor maltings and a stone
warehouse. Almost all casks used are ex-sherry casks, giving a
rich berry flavour.
CAPACITY IN MILLION LITRES: 1.4
WHAT TO LOOK FOR: Glendronach 12-year-old; Glendronach 33-
year-old; Vintage 1968
Open to visitors

Glendullan (18)
Dufftown, Banffshire. Tel 01340 822100 www.malts.com
Built by a firm of blenders in 1897, this distillery was the
last of seven to be built in Dufftown. It is not well known
for its single malt, although Betty Boothroyd, former
Speaker of the House of Commons, chose it as the Speaker's
whisky in 1992.
CAPACITY IN MILLION LITRES: 3.7
WHAT TO LOOK FOR: Glendullan 12-year-old; Glendullan Rare Malt

Glen Elgin (19)
Longmorn, Elgin, Morayshire. Tel 01343 862100
www.malts.com
Although established over 100 years ago, in 1900, the malt
was only bottled as a single malt in 1970. Six worm tubs
produce whisky slowly and with character. Most is used in
the White Horse blend.
CAPACITY IN MILLION LITRES: 1.5
WHAT TO LOOK FOR: Glen Elgin 12-year-old; Glen Elgin
32-year-old

Glenfarclas (20)

Ballindalloch, Banffshire. Tel 01807 500209
www.scotchwhisky.net
Another traditional distillery, producing robust malt, aged in sherry casks. Founded in 1836, it has remained in the Grant family since 1865. The firm was shipping Pure Old Glenfarcas Glenlivet to the US in 1899. Glenfarclas 105 is 60% proof, one of the strongest on the market. The Family Casks 1952–1994 are 2008 award winners (*Jim Murray's Bible* Awards).
CAPACITY IN MILLION LITRES: 3
WHAT TO LOOK FOR: Glenfarclas 10-, 12-, 15-, 21-, 25- and 30-year-olds; Glenfarclas 105
Open to visitors

Glenfiddich (21)

Dufftown, Banffshire. Tel 01340 820373
www.glenfiddich.com
Founded by William Grant in 1887, using equipment from Elizabeth Cummings at Cardhu for £120, this is the name which was the first to promote single malt for the mass market. In the 1960s Grant opened a centre for visitors and shared the secrets of malt. It has remained the world's biggest seller as a result. There are 29 stills, modelled on Cardhu. On the same site as Balvenie, Glenfiddich is often considered a beginner's malt. The triangular bottle was designed to fit neatly into a briefcase and not to roll about.
CAPACITY IN MILLION LITRES: 10
WHAT TO LOOK FOR: Caoran Reserve 12-year-old; Special Reserve 12-year-old; Solera Reserve 15-year-old; Ancient Reserve 18-year-old; Glenfiddich 30-year-old
Open to visitors

Glen Grant (22)

Rothes, Morayshire. Tel 01542 783318
www.scotchwhisky.net
This sounds like my sort of place: a distillery for garden lovers — two for the price of one!
This malt is popular in Europe, especially in Italy, but not well known at home. The taste is said to be clean and apple-like.
CAPACITY IN MILLION LITRES: 5.4
WHAT TO LOOK FOR: Glen Grant 5- and 10-year-olds; Lord of the Isles
Open to visitors

Glenlivet (23)

Ballindalloch, Banffshire. Tel 01542 783220
www.theglenlivet.com
By 1871, this was the best-known distillery in Scotland.
The name was adopted by at least 10 other distilleries in
the glen, as everyone jumped on the bandwagon. This was
the first licensed distillery in Speyside, leased by George
Smith from the Duke of Gordon. This was the whisky
demanded by George IV in 1822. Twice a year whisky is
distilled, as it was 200 years ago, and the visitor centre is
highly recommended.
CAPACITY IN MILLION LITRES: 5.5
WHAT TO LOOK FOR: The Glenlivet 12-year-old; The Glenlivet
15-year-old; French Oak Reserve; The Glenlivet 18-year-old;
Nadurra 16-year-old
Open to visitors

Glenlossie (24)

Elgin, Morayshire. Tel 01343 86200
www.malts.com
This distillery is next door to Mannochmore, and shares the
same workforce. It operates for part of the year only, but
produces outstanding-quality malt, perhaps because of the
purifiers on its three spirit stills. Built close to the railway, it
had its own sidings and relied on water power until the 1960s.
CAPACITY IN MILLION LITRES: 1.1
WHAT TO LOOK FOR: Glenlossie 10-year-old

Glen Moray (25)

Elgin, Morayshire. Tel 01343 550900 www.glenmoray.com
This small distillery offers visits where you can see the
whisky maturing inside the casks, thanks to the wonders of
Perspex ends. The maturing fruit and honey malt becomes
more apparent as the colour develops. The range also
includes vintages and distiller's choices.
CAPACITY IN MILLION LITRES: 1.85
WHAT TO LOOK FOR: Glen Moray Classic; Glen Moray 12- and 16-
year-olds; 1991 Mountain Oak Malt
Open to visitors

Glenrothes (26)

Rothes, Morayshire. Tel 01340 872300
www.glenrotheswhisky.com
This distillery, dating from 1878, is one of the larger
Speysiders, with 10 stills. It produces malt for several
blends, including Cutty Sark. Single malt comes in dumpy
bottles with handwritten-style labelling.

CAPACITY IN MILLION LITRES: 5.6

WHAT TO LOOK FOR: The Glenrothes Select Reserve and Vintages
Visitors by appointment only

Glen Spey (27)

Rothes, Morayshire. Tel 01340 831215 www.malts.com
Most of the malt from here goes to blends, especially for
J&B, although there are rare releases available. Founded in
1884, it was sold to Gilbey, the London-based gin people,
soon afterwards. Glen Spey thus became known in London
society early on.

CAPACITY IN MILLION LITRES: 1.4

WHAT TO LOOK FOR: Glen Spey Flora and Fauna 12-year-old

Glentauchters (28)

Mulben, Keith, Banffshire. Tel 01542 860272
www.scotchwhisky.net
This large distillery's output nearly all goes for blending in
Ballantine's. It was built in 1897, to serve the needs of
Buchanan's blend of Black and White.

CAPACITY IN MILLION LITRES: 3.4

WHAT TO LOOK FOR: Glentauchers 14-year-old

Inchgower (29)

Buckie, Banffshire. Tel 01542 836700
www.malts.com
Most malt goes to Bell's and Johnny Walker blends. The coastal
positioning means that this is not a typical Speyside malt.

CAPACITY IN MILLION LITRES: 2.2

WHAT TO LOOK FOR: Inchgower Flora and Fauna 14-year-old
range; 22-year-old Rare Malt; 27-year-old Rare Malt

Kininvie (30)
Dufftown, Morayshire.
www.scotchwhisky.net
This distillery is hidden behind Glenfiddich and Balvenie, and produces malt for William Grant & Son blends, such as Monkey Shoulder. It was opened in 1990.
CAPACITY IN MILLION LITRES: —
WHAT TO LOOK FOR: Not yet available

Knockando (31)
Knockando, Aberlour, Morayshire. Tel 01340 882000
www.malts.com
This malt is widely marketed in the US and Europe, although it is less well known at home. It is used in J&B blends.
CAPACITY IN MILLION LITRES: 1.3
WHAT TO LOOK FOR: Knockando 18-year-old

Knockdhu (32)
Knock, Huntley, Aberdeenshire. Tel 01466 771223
www.inverhouse.com
Not to be confused with Knockando, this large distillery produces a high proportion of single malt. It is often thought to be more like Highland malt than a Speyside.
CAPACITY IN MILLION LITRES: N/A
WHAT TO LOOK FOR: Linkwood 12-year-old
Open to visitors

Linkwood (33)
Elgin, Morayshire. Tel 01343 862000
www.malts.com
Another idyllic place: a distillery surrounded by a nature reserve. Started up in 1820 by a local farmer, it has two sets of stills which are mixed before casking. It is popular with blenders, though there are some malts around.
CAPACITY IN MILLION LITRES: 3
WHAT TO LOOK FOR: Linkwood 12-year-old

Longmorn (34)
Elgin, Morayshire. Tel 01542 783042
This enjoys a cult following and opens, on occasions, for
festivals. An older sister to Ben Riach, it was built four
years before, in 1894. Longmorn 16-year-old is 48% proof,
so it packs quite a punch.
CAPACITY IN MILLION LITRES: 3.3
WHAT TO LOOK FOR: Longmorn 16-year-old; 17-year-old
Distiller's Edition

Macallan (35)
Craigellachie, Morayshire. 01340 872280
www.the macallan.com
Established well before licensing in 1815, this estate overlooks
the River Spey. It was a farm with a still and a staging post for
cattle drovers, so it was ideally placed for picking up some
whisky in passing. Small, squat stills make a lot of whisky, and
the visitor centre explains the role played by wood.
CAPACITY IN MILLION LITRES: 6
WHAT TO LOOK FOR: The Macallan Fine Oak range 10-, 15-, 21-
and 30-year-olds; The Macallan Sherry Oak 10-, 12-, 15-, 21-
and 30-year-olds; Elegancia

Macduff (36)
Macduff, Banffshire. Tel 01261 812612
www.scotchwhisky.net
Just to confuse you, this distillery bottles under the name
of the local river, Glen Deveron. It was opened in the 1960s
for blending stock, but some now finds its way onto the
market as a single malt.
CAPACITY IN MILLION LITRES: 2.4
WHAT TO LOOK FOR: Glen Deveron 10- and 15-year-olds

Mannochmore (37)
Elgin, Morayshire. Tel 01343 862000
www.malts.com
Established in 1971, to provide malt for the Haig blend, a
single malt called Loch Dhu, a black whisky, has some
followers as a collectable.
CAPACITY IN MILLION LITRES: 1.3
WHAT TO LOOK FOR: Mannochmore 12-year-old; Loch Dhu

Miltonduff (38)
Elgin, Morayshire. Tel 01343 547433 www.scotchwhisky.net
Ballantine's receives most of the malt produced here.
Established in 1824, inside an old priory brewing house, the
source of water for the ale is still the same as that used for
whisky distillation.

CAPACITY IN MILLION LITRES: 5.2

WHAT TO LOOK FOR: Miltonduff 12-year-old

Mortlach (39)
Dufftown, Banffshire. Tel 01340 822100 www.malts.com
After a faltering start in 1824, this became one of the
biggest distilleries in Scotland. William Grant was
bookkeeper here before building Glenfiddich. Partially triple
distilled, this whisky has an unusual oily taste for a
Speyside. It is used in blending, as it is said to complement
lots of other flavours.

CAPACITY IN MILLION LITRES: 2.8

WHAT TO LOOK FOR: Mortlach 16-year-old

Speyburn (40)
Rothes, Morayshire. Tel 01340 831213 www.inverhouse.com
Dating from 1897, most of the malt is exported to the
US, although recently Speyburn 10-year-old has been
making waves.

CAPACITY IN MILLION LITRES: 1

WHAT TO LOOK FOR: Speyburn 10- and 25-year-olds
Visitors by appointment only

Speyside (41)
Kingussie, Inverness-shire. Tel 01540 661060
www.speysidedistillery.co.uk
Also known as Drumguish, this is a new, small distillery to
the south of the area, founded in 1990. It was used for
filming the *Monarch of the Glen* TV series. The company
that owns it has its own bottling and blending business in
Glasgow.

CAPACITY IN MILLION LITRES: 0.6

WHAT TO LOOK FOR: Speyside 8-, 10- and 12-year-olds;
Drumguish

Strathisla (42)

Keith, Banffshire. Tel 01542 783044 www.chivas.com
This is the oldest working plant in the Highlands, founded in
1786. The pagoda roofs add to its charm. Water comes from
a well first used by brewers of heather ales during the 11th
century. It plays a key role in producing Chivas blends.
CAPACITY IN MILLION LITRES: 2
WHAT TO LOOK FOR: Strathisla 12- and 18-year-olds; Strathisla
15-year-old Cask Strength
Open to visitors

Strathmill (43)

Keith, Banffshire. Tel 01542 883000 www.malts.com
Another distillery with twin pagodas, Strathmill produces
light whiskies, greatly in demand for blending. J&B use a
lot. It was built on the site of an old grain mill, in 1891.
CAPACITY IN MILLION LITRES: 1.7
WHAT TO LOOK FOR: Strathmill 12-year-old

Tamdhu (44)

Knockando, Aberlour, Morayshire. Tel 01340 870221
www.edringtongroup.com
Famous Grouse uses a lot of the malt in its blends. Set up in
1897, on the Strathspey railway (1863), it is well placed for
transport and spring water from the Knockando Burn. It still
provides malt for other distilleries.
CAPACITY IN MILLION LITRES: 4
WHAT TO LOOK FOR: Tamdhu 29-year-old

Tomintoul (45)

Ballindalloch, Banffshire. Tel 01807 590274
www.tomintouldistillery.com
Established in 1961, the highest village in the Highlands
houses this large producer. It is used in the Whyte & Mackay
blend and also bottled as a single malt.
CAPACITY IN MILLION LITRES: 3
WHAT TO LOOK FOR: Tomintoul 10-, 16- and 27-year-olds

Tormore (46)
Advie, Grantown-on-Spey, Morayshire. Tel 01807 510244
www.tormore.com
This showcase distillery was built in the 1950s by American
producers. Although that doesn't mean that it is open to
visitors, it does have a chiming clock playing 'Highland
Laddie' every hour! The malt goes mainly to Ballantine's
and Teachers.
CAPACITY IN MILLION LITRES: 3.5
WHAT TO LOOK FOR: Tormore 12-year-old

DISTILLERIES NOW CLOSED OR MOTHBALLED IN SPEYSIDE
Although these are closed, you may still come across
some of the malt — at a price!

- Banff
- Braeval
- Caperdonach
- Coleburn
- Convalmore
- Dallas Dhu
- Glenlassaugh
- Glen Keith
- Imperial
- Pittyvaich
- Tamnavulin

VISITING EXPERIENCES IN SPEYSIDE

Dallas Dhu
Forres Morayshire. Tel 01309 676548
www.historic-scotland.gov.uk

This former distillery now runs as a museum, and is
open all the year round.

Spirit of Speyside Whisky Festival
Details of forthcoming festivals are available at:
www.spiritofspeyside.com

THE HIGHLANDS

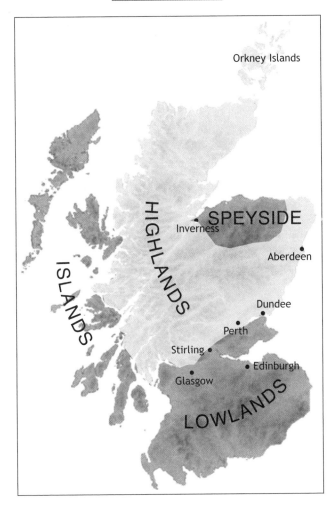

The Highlands region stretches northwards from the Firth of Clyde in the west to the coast below Aberdeen in the east. The geography of the Highland region as well as historical events have created the current picture. Don't forget, either, that the Speyside region falls within the Highlands. Two huge fault lines, resulting from violent activity below the Earth's crust, have shaped the region we see today.

On top of that, 400 million years of weathering have had a massive effect on the erosion of mountains thrown up at the time of faulting. So, the physical boundaries are hard to miss, but events in the past have also highlighted the differences between Highland producers and those of the Lowlands. The 18th-century lawmakers recognised that conditions were much tougher in the north and that yields of crops were lower, so they charged less duty than on Lowland producers. As a sweetener to the south, Highland whisky was not allowed to leave the Highlands. Local methods, combined with longer winters and isolation, meant that whisky became part of the culture, in the same way as music and tartan. Many producers benefited from the allowance on duty, and, after the construction of grain distilleries for continuous production in the south, the Highlands became the 'spiritual' home of single malt.

As a general rule — which will no doubt be shot down by real enthusiasts and experts — Highland malts tend to be more robust than Lowland malts and not as heathery or sweet as Speyside malts. There may be an element of smokiness, but this is not as strong as the Islay malts. That said, there are, of course, coastal distilleries which have a salty tang, as well. The Orkney distilleries are included in the Highlands group.

KEY TO MAP (page 79)
(1) Aberfeldy
(2) Ardmore
(3) Balblair
(4) Ben Nevis
(5) Blair Athol
(6) Clynelish
(7) Dalmore
(8) Dalwhinnie
(9) Deanston
(10) Edradour
(11) Fettercairn
(12) Glencadam
(13) Glen Garioch
(14) Glengoyne
(15) Glenmorangie
(16) Glen Ord
(17) Glenturret
(18) Highland Park
(19) Loch Lomond
(20) Oban
(21) Old Pulteney
(22) Royal Brackla
(23) Royal Lochnagar
(24) Scapa
(25) Teaninich
(26) Tomatin
(27) Tullibardine

DISTILLERIES OF THE HIGHLANDS REGION

There seem to be a lot more distilleries geared up for visitors in the Highlands, which is obviously good for tourism.

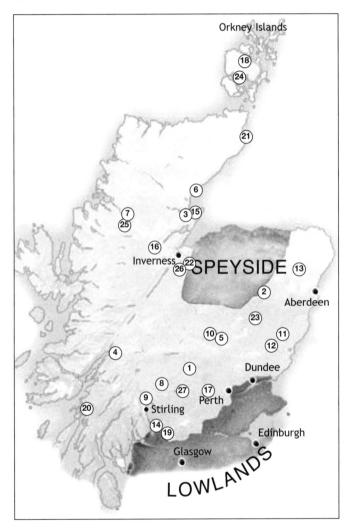

Aberfeldy (1)
Aberfeldy, Perthshire. Tel 01877 822010
www.aberfeldy.com
www.dewarsworldofwhisky.com
Here you can combine a visit to a distillery with Dewar's
World of Whisky, which celebrates, unsurprisingly, the
Dewar's brand. Built in 1898 by John Dewar, it was,
nevertheless, his sons who made the brand famous.
CAPACITY IN MILLION LITRES: 1.8
WHAT TO LOOK FOR: Aberfeldy 12-year-old; Aberfeldy
21-year-old
Open to visitors

Ardmore (2)
Kennethmont, Huntley, Aberdeenshire. Tel 01464 831213
www.scotchwhisky.net
Established in 1989, it was founded by Adam Teacher, who
moved from selling bottled malt to drams over the counter,
which, by the 1860s, were mostly blends. Now producing
mainly for Teacher's, although some is available as single
malt.
CAPACITY IN MILLION LITRES: 5
WHAT TO LOOK FOR: Ardmore Traditional Cask 46%

Balblair (3)
Edderton, Ross-shire. Tel 01862 821273
www.inverhouse.com
This distillery was first built in 1790, although whisky was
made here in the 17th century. It was rebuilt in 1872, next
to the railway. Close to Glenmorangie, the pure air is said
to be reflected in the purity of the single malt, which is
sold in distinctively shaped bottles.
CAPACITY IN MILLION LITRES: 1.3
WHAT TO LOOK FOR: Balblair 1977, 1979, 1989 and 1997
Open to visitors

Ben Nevis (4)
Lochy Bridge, Fort William, Inverness-shire.
Tel 01397 700200   www.bennevisdistillery.com
With no other distilleries for 50 miles and situated beneath
the mountain, this distillery is often visited. It was built in
1825 and is now Japanese owned. Bottles of single malt and
blended whisky are sold under the same name.
CAPACITY IN MILLION LITRES: 2
WHAT TO LOOK FOR: Ben Nevis 10-year-old; 13-year-old Ort
Finish; Glencoe Blend 8-year-old
Open to visitors

Blair Athol (5)
Pitlochry, Perthshire. Tel 01796 482003
www.discoveringdistilleries.com
Established in 1798, the original distillery floundered, but
when Arthur Bell's family moved to Perth in the 1820s, he
joined a wine and spirit merchants and started to buy
whisky for the firm. He later started his blending business
with whisky from Blair Athol. Not much is bottled now as
malt, and most goes to Bell's blends.
CAPACITY IN MILLION LITRES: 2
WHAT TO LOOK FOR: Blair Athol 12-year-old
Open to visitors

Clynelish (6)
Brora, Sutherland. Tel 01408 623000 www.malts.com
This remote, seaside distillery produces rich, smoky, salty
malt. The current distillery dates from 1967, but the
original Clynelish dates from 1896. This was finally closed in
1983; it was briefly named Brora. The water from the
Clynemilton Burn runs over rocks containing gold.
CAPACITY IN MILLION LITRES: 3.4
WHAT TO LOOK FOR: Clynelish 14-year-old
Open to visitors

Dalmore (7)
Alness, Ross-shire. Tel 01349 882362
www.thedalmore.com
This remote, eastern Highland coastal distillery is situated
on the banks of the Cromarty Firth. Some of its oldest
whiskies have changed hands for big, big money at auction.
Established in 1839, much of the malt goes into Whyte and
Mackay blends. The distinctive bottle is bell-shaped.
CAPACITY IN MILLION LITRES: 3.2
WHAT TO LOOK FOR: Dalmore 12-year-old; 21-year-old The Cigar
Malt; Dalmore 1973
Open to visitors

Dalwhinnie (8)
Dalwhinnie, Inverness-shire. Tel 01540 672219
www.malts.com
Founded in 1897, this is the highest distillery, and is
situated in the coldest inhabited place in Scotland, with a
mean annual temperature of 6°C. The weather is great for
the whisky. Cool, fresh water flowing from the Drumochter
Hills and a nearby railway line are real bonuses.
CAPACITY IN MILLION LITRES: 1.3
WHAT TO LOOK FOR: Dalwhinnie 15-year-old 43%
Open to visitors

Deanston (9)
Doune, Perthshire. Tel 01786 841422
www.burnstewartdistillers.com
Founded in 1966, the building was once a cotton mill designed
by James Arkwright. Most of the malt goes to Scottish Leader
blended whisky. Single malt from Tobermory is matured here.
CAPACITY IN MILLION LITRES: 3
WHAT TO LOOK FOR: Deanston 12-year-old; 30-year-old Limited
Edition

Edradour (10)
Pitlochry, Perthshire. Tel 01796 472095
www.edradour.co.uk
Near Blair Athol, so quite accessible. Established in 1825, this very small distillery is a popular visitor attraction. It produces only about 12 casks per week, so is not easily found. Independently owned, it produces unusual whiskies bottled straight from the cask. 200,000 bottles went down with a ship in 1941, off the outer Hebrides, inspiring Compton Mackenzie's story *Whisky Galore*.
CAPACITY IN MILLION LITRES: 0.9
WHAT TO LOOK FOR: Edradour 10-year-old; Straight from the Cask; Edradour 30-year-old
Open to visitors

Fettercairn (11)
Laurencekirk, Kincardineshire. Tel 01561 340205
www.whyteand mackay.co.uk
In prime barley country, this distillery is one of the few survivors on the east coast. A converted grain mill, it opened in 1824. Owned by Americans for many years, most of the malt now goes into the Whyte and Mackay blends. It is not as heavy as other Highland malts.
CAPACITY IN MILLION LITRES: 1.6
WHAT TO LOOK FOR: Fettercairn 1824 12-year-old
Open to visitors

Glencadam (12)
Brechin, Angus.   Tel 01356 622217 www.angusdundee.co.uk
Originally opened in 1825, this is the only distillery left in Angus. Closed in 2000 and reopened in 2003, it produces malt for blends for Balantine's, Teacher's and Stewart's Cream of the Barley, as well as 15-year-old single malt.
CAPACITY IN MILLION LITRES: 1.5
WHAT TO LOOK FOR: Glencadam 15-year-old
Open to visitors

Glen Garioch (13)
Meldrum, Aberdeenshire.   Tel 01651 873450
www.glengarioch.com
Built in 1798, this producer still has some of the original
buildings intact. Pronounced 'Glen Geery', it produced
robust, peaty malt for Vat 69. The peat has now been
reduced. Heat from the kilns is diverted into heating
greenhouses, which grow tomatoes on a commercial scale.
CAPACITY IN MILLION LITRES: 1
WHAT TO LOOK FOR: Glen Garioch 8-, 15- and 21-year-olds; Glen
Garioch 46-year-old
Open to visitors

Glengoyne (14)
Drumgoyne, Killearn, Glasgow.   Tel 01360 550254
www.glengoyne.com
This distillery was the first Highland distillery, and was
known as Burnfoot. Built on Campsie Fell, it is just over the
Highland Line or border, in country which was once rife with
smuggling and cattle rustling, Rob Roy style. Rebuilt and
modernised in the 1960s, it uses Scottish oak casks. A four-
hour masterclass is offered to visitors, as well as other
tours.
CAPACITY IN MILLION LITRES: 1.2
WHAT TO LOOK FOR: Glengoyne 10-, 17-, 21- and 28-year-olds;
Cask Strength 12-year-old
Open to visitors

Glenmorangie (15)
Tain, Ross-shire. Tel 01862 892477 www.glenmorangie.com
Established in 1843, this very popular single malt is a giant
among Scotch. Most goes straight into single malts. A small
amount of Glen Moray, the sister distillery, is added to
every cask traded. The east coast setting gives a fresh,
gentle, smoky flavour. Glenmorangie Nectar D'Or was voted
World's Best Highland Single Malt Whisky for 2008 by *Whisky
Magazine*.
CAPACITY IN MILLION LITRES: 2.9
WHAT TO LOOK FOR: Glenmorangie 10-year-old Original Artisan
Cask; Glenmorangie 18- and 25-year-olds; Nectar D'Or 46%;
Lasanta 46%
Open to visitors

Glen Ord (16)
Muir of Ord, Ross-shire. Tel 01463 872004
www.discoveringdistilleries.com
Built within a few miles of Ferintosh, Glen Ord has had
mixed fortunes. Stocks amounting to 8 million gallons were
transferred to Dewar's and Johnny Walker, in the 1920s.
Mothballed during World War II and expanded in the 1960s
to fulfil world-wide demand, this distillery now has its own
modern maltings.
CAPACITY IN MILLION LITRES: 3.4
WHAT TO LOOK FOR: Glen Ord 12-year-old
Open to visitors

Glenturret (17)
Crieff, Perthshire. Tel 01764 656565
www.famousgrouse.co.uk
For a small distillery, this one gets a lot of visitors. Founded
in 1775, most of the malt goes to The Famous Grouse blend,
but vatted malts are available. The Famous Grouse
Experience is an interactive visitor attraction, which is
highly recommended.
CAPACITY IN MILLION LITRES: 0.34
WHAT TO LOOK FOR: Glenturret 10-year-old
Open to visitors

Highland Park (18)
Kirkwall, Orkney.   Tel 01856 874619
www.highlandpark.co.uk
This distillery began life in 1798, and is now the most
northerly distillery in the UK. The most notorious smuggler
on Orkney, Magnus Eunson, was also the minister of the
Kirk. He once hid barrels of malt under a coffin lid and
sheet, to put off excise men. The congregation apparently
saw them off by muttering about smallpox! Eunson used
water from springs in the high park, giving the distillery its
name. One fifth of the barley is still malted on site, and
peat is locally cut, giving a smoky, heathery, honey flavour.
CAPACITY IN MILLION LITRES: 2.5
WHAT TO LOOK FOR: Highland Park 12-, 15-, 16-, 18-, 25- and
30-year-olds
Open to visitors

Loch Lomond (19)
Alexandria, Dumbartonshire.   Tel 01389 752781
www.lochlomonddistillery.com
This distillery is the odd one out. It has pot stills and a
grain still, making a range of different styles for blends.
Some single malts are also produced.
CAPACITY IN MILLION LITRES: 2.5 (malt and grain)
WHAT TO LOOK FOR: Loch Lomond; Old Rhosdhu 5-year-old;
Inchmurrin

Oban (20)
Oban, Argyll. Tel 01631 572004
www.malts.com
The distillery is situated in the town, although it was once
by the water's edge, as the sea has receded. Whisky has
been made here, more or less continuously, since 1794.
During work in 1890 to enlarge storage by blasting into a
rockface, Walter Higgins found evidence of the Scoti, a
tribe of ancient cave dwellers dating from 5000 BC.
CAPACITY IN MILLION LITRES: 0.7
WHAT TO LOOK FOR: Oban 14- and 32-year-olds; Oban 1980
Distiller's Edition Double Matured
Open to visitors

Old Pulteney (21)
Wick, Caithness.   Tel 01955 602371 www.oldpulteney.com
Founded in 1826, 29 km (18 miles) from John O'Groats.
Wick was once a fishing boom town, where Sir William
Pulteney made his money from herrings. In 1922, Wick
became one of 56 Temperance towns. You could say they
were truly high and dry! After 1945, production continued.
The peculiar shaped wash stills perhaps account for the
clean, aromatic spirit produced.
CAPACITY IN MILLION LITRES: 1
WHAT TO LOOK FOR: Old Pulteney 12- and 21-year-olds; Old
Pulteney 17-year-old 46%
Open to visitors

Royal Brackla (22)
Cawdor, Nairn, Nairnshire. Tel 01667 402002
www.scotchwhisky.net
Founded in 1812, the distillery gained the patronage of
William IV after licensing. This was later extended by Queen
Victoria. Modernisation in the 1970s added extra stills.
CAPACITY IN MILLION LITRES: 2.5
WHAT TO LOOK FOR: Royal Brackla 10-year-old

Royal Lochnagar (23)
Crathie, Ballater, Aberdeenshire. Tel 01339 742700
www.malts.com
Just a mile from Balmoral, this distillery was originally set
up in 1825, and rebuilt as New Lochnagar in 1845. Visited
by Queen Victoria, Prince Albert and the family, in 1848, as
recorded by John Beggs, it achieved Royal status in 1851. It
was used in Vat 69, and now features in Johnny Walker blue
and gold label blends.
CAPACITY IN MILLION LITRES: 0.4
WHAT TO LOOK FOR: Royal Lochnagar 12-year-old Limited
Edition; Selected Reserve; Royal Lochnagar
Open to visitors

Scapa (24)
St Ola, Kirkwall, Orkney. Tel 01856 872071
www.scapamalt.com
Close to Highland Park and opened in 1885. It had a ringside
seat when the German fleet was scuttled at the end of
World War I. Two stills and a short distillation season make
this a rare malt, salt flecked and heathery in taste.
CAPACITY IN MILLION LITRES: 1
WHAT TO LOOK FOR: Scapa 14-year-old

Teaninich (25)
Alness, Ross-shire. Tel 01349 885001 www.malts.com
Dating from 1817, this distillery was last modernised in the
1970s. There are two distilleries on site, and the malt is
vatted together.
CAPACITY IN MILLION LITRES: 2.5
WHAT TO LOOK FOR: Teaninich 10-year-old

Tomatin (26)
Tomatin, Inverness-shire. Tel 01808 511444
www.tomatin.com
Built in 1897, this is now a giant distillery with 23 stills. It
became the first one to be Japanese owned, in the 1980s. It
supplies blends for Big T and makes a toffee-scented,
peppery malt.
CAPACITY IN MILLION LITRES: 5
WHAT TO LOOK FOR: Tomatin 12-year-old
Open to visitors

Tullibardine (27)
Blackford, Perthshire. Tel 01764 682252
www.tullibardine.com
This distillery was mothballed for nine years until 2003, and
malt was not produced for a number of years. Beer was
brewed on this site 500 years ago. It is part of a shopping
complex, attracting tourists on the A9.
CAPACITY IN MILLION LITRES: 2
WHAT TO LOOK FOR: Tullibardine 10-year-old
Open to visitors

HIGHLAND DISTILLERIES NOW CLOSED OR MOTHBALLED

You may still come across some of these names,
again, at a price!

• Ben Wyvis
• Brora
• Glen Albyn
• Glenesk/Hillside
• Glenlochy
• Glen Mhor
• Glenugie
• Glenury Royal
• Lochside
• Millburn
• North Port/Brechin

OTHER PLACES TO VISIT

Dewar's World of Whisky, Aberfeldy
www.dewarswow.com

The Famous Grouse Experience
Glenturret Distillery, Crieff, Perthshire
www.famousgrouse.co.uk

THE ISLANDS

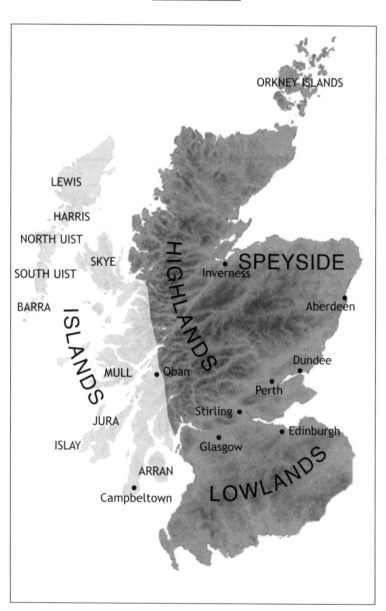

Here you'll find the oldest rocks in Britain, dating from 3 billion years ago. The region includes the islands of the Hebrides, Skye, Mull and Islay, as well as Campbeltown. The latter isn't an island but a peninsular, so, literally, almost an island. Even within such a limited area, there are distinctive differences, and it is interesting that three of the four new distilleries opening in Scotland are in this area. A high proportion of recent award winning whiskies come from this region, considering that this is a small area.

Some 60 million years ago there was intense volcanic activity. As the lava cooled it became black basalt, forming the Giant's Causeway off Northern Ireland and Fingal's Cave off the Isle of Mull, so Mull shares quite a lot, geologically, with the coast of Northern Ireland and the water which feeds Tobermory flows over the same type of rocks as the water feeding Bushmill's in County Antrim (see Irish Distilleries page 108).

It isn't just the remoteness of the region and its geology that have made Island whisky so distinct: a very bloody history has also had an influence. In 1493, the king of Scotland forced the head of the MacDonald clan to give up his title of 'Lord of the Isles', starting inter-clan warfare which lasted for 100 years. There was a huge amount of drink-fuelled violence going on during this time, and imported liquor was banned, to try to stop the carnage. In 1614, the MacDonalds finally lost their power base on Islay, although one clan chief was given an allowance of 18 bottles per day on Mull. Martin Martin wrote *A Description of the Western Isles*, around 1695, and spoke of *Usquebaugh* and *Usquebaugh-baul*, *'which at first taste affects all the Members of the Body. Two spoonfuls is a sufficient Dose and if any Man exceed this, it would presently stop his Breath and endanger his Life.'*

This brew was made from oats, he thought, although wheat and other grains were also used. No wonder there was such a lot of bad behaviour! Even by 1838, when Samuel Moorwood wrote *Inebriating Liquors*, things hadn't got much better. He described how a goblet or shell of whisky would be passed round and round the company until it was all gone, or until everyone had collapsed. Actually, that sounds more like a student party I remember from the 1970s!

The poor quality of soil on all but Islay and Tiree encouraged the growing of crops rather than the rearing of animals. Of every harvest of barley, at least a third was distilled during the 18th century. Farming on Islay developed at this time, when a new strain of barley was introduced. Whisky distillation depended on the quality of the harvest and, in poor years, there was a conflict between making spirit and feeding people. There were no excise men on Islay until 1797 and even then they needed protection from the militia, which is not surprising, having described the scenes above!

Grain imports began after 1815, and there were 21 licensed distilleries, at one point, on the Isle of Islay alone. Islay malts are identified by their heavy peatiness: rich in bog myrtle, moss and brine. The peat is laid over coke in malting kilns in Port Ellen. Almost all Islay malt is now matured in warehouses in the Lowlands, under controlled conditions. There are now nine distilleries on Islay, including the new Kilchoman Distillery and Port Charlotte. Islay whiskies are the strongest flavoured of all malt whiskies, being heavily influenced by their physical location. You either love them or hate them. As a novice, I haven't learned to love them yet, but have a good friend who has raved about Laphroaig for years. Islay is very much peat and water, with the burns having a distinctive brown hue. Winter gales drive salt spray inland, which saturates the peat. The distilleries on the south of the island, Ardbeg, Lagavulin and Laphroaig, produce whiskies with a stronger, peaty flavour. On the north side are Bowmore, Bruichladdich, Bunnahabhain and Caol Ila, with a lighter taste.

ISLAND DISTILLERIES

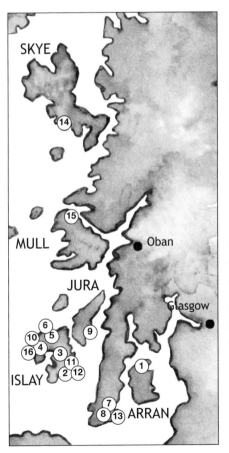

KEY TO MAP
(1) Arran
(2) Ardbeg
(3) Bowmore
(4) Bruichladdich
(5) Bunnahabhain
(6) Caol Ila
(7) Glengyle
(8) Glen Scotia
(9) Jura
(10) Kilchoman
(11) Lagavulin
(12) Laphroaig
(13) Springbank
(14) Talisker
(15) Tobermory
(16) Port Charlotte

Arran (1)
Lochranza, Arran. Tel 01786 431900 www.arranwhisky.com
Opened as recently as 1995, this distillery has quite a few
achievements already, named Distillery of the Year by
Whisky Magazine in 2007 and scooping Best Single Malt (12
years and under) in *Jim Murray's Whisky Bible* Awards 2008.
CAPACITY IN MILLION LITRES: 0.75
WHAT TO LOOK FOR: Arran 10-year-old; The Arran Malt; Arran
100 proof; Robert Burns Single Malt
Open to visitors

Ardbeg (2)
Port Ellen, Islay. Tel 01496 302244
www.ardbeg.com
Ardbeg began as an illicit still, well before licensing in
1815. The sea comes right up to the distillery walls here,
and the whisky is very peaty, oily and tangy. Jim Murray's
Whisky Bible announced Ardbeg 10-year-old as Scotch Single
Malt and World Whisky of the Year for 2008. It helps,
considerably, if you like peated malt.
CAPACITY IN MILLION LITRES: 1
WHAT TO LOOK FOR: Ardberg 10; 17-year-old Kildalton;
Provenance 1974; Uigeadail; Airigh Man Beist; Lord of
the Isles
Open to visitors

Bowmore (3)
Bowmore, Islay. Tel 01496 810441
www.bowmore.com
Bowmore has its own maltings and peat-burning fires. The
malt has a distinctive taste, not appreciated by my French
neighbour, who thought there was something medicinal
about it. He didn't like it with cola, either! At least it isn't
fishy!
CAPACITY IN MILLION LITRES: 2
WHAT TO LOOK FOR: Bowmore 12-, 15-, 18- and 25-year-olds
Open to visitors

Bruichladdich (4)

Bruichladdich, Islay. Tel 01496 850221
www. bruichladdich.com
Reopened in 2001 by an independent bottler, this distillery doesn't supply for blends, so there is more for single malt, which is aged, on site, before going for bottling. Even then, Islay water is used to dilute the spirit to 46% abv.

CAPACITY IN MILLION LITRES: 1.5

WHAT TO LOOK FOR: Bruichladdich 10-, 12- and 15-year-olds; Bruichladdich XVII

Open to visitors

Bunnahabhain (5)

Port Askaig, Islay. Tel 01496 840646
www.bunnahabhain.com
Pronounced Boona *hav* en, this unpeated, but still salty, whisky is growing in popularity. The 25-year-old malt was voted World's Best Islay Unpeated Single Malt in 2008, by *Whisky Magazine*, although there can't be that many contenders.

CAPACITY IN MILLION LITRES: 2.5

WHAT TO LOOK FOR: Bunnahabhain 12-, 18- and 25-year-olds

Open to visitors

Caol Ila (6)

Port Askaig, Islay. Tel 01496 302760
www.malts.com
This is the biggest producer on Islay, although probably not the best known, as a lot of the malt goes to blends like Johnny Walker's. Refurbished in the 1970s, it doesn't have a lot of charm about it, but it has been around since 1846. In the 1880s, it had two steamers per week delivering grain and taking away casks of whisky. The taste is said to be robust, strongly peated and oily with a hint of grilled fish or bacon about it. That's the main course dealt with, then: what's for pudding?

CAPACITY IN MILLION LITRES: 3.6

WHAT TO LOOK FOR: Caol Ila 12-, 18- and 25-year-olds; Caol Ila Cask Strength

Open to visitors

Glengyle (7)

Campbeltown, Argyll. Tel 01586 552009

www.kikerran.com

This new distillery is on the site of a former still built by a local farmer in 1872. William Mitchell and his brother fell out over sheep, however, and the entire stock was sold off in 1925. By 1970, Glengyle was just a farm again, but in 2000, Hedley Wright, a distant relative of the Mitchells, formed a new company, with stills and condensers from Ben Wyvis. Opened in 2004, the first spirit reached the magic age of three in April 2007. It will be known as Kilkerran.

CAPACITY IN MILLION LITRES: New distillery

Open to visitors

Glen Scotia (8)

Campbeltown, Argyll. Tel 01586 552288

www.lochlomonddistillery.com

Campbeltown used to be a vibrant whisky town with 34 distilleries until Speyside took over as the whisky centre; by 1930 there were only two left. Glen Scotia, started in 1832, has had several periods of resting. It is one of Scotland's smallest distilleries.

CAPACITY IN MILLION LITRES: 0.75

WHAT TO LOOK FOR: Glen Scotia 12- and 17-year-olds

Jura (9)

Craighouse, Isle of Jura. Tel 01496 820385

www.isleof jura.com

This was founded in 1810 and rebuilt in the 1950s. In 2007, the distillery was bought by an Indian entrepreneur and it produces a highly peated malt.

CAPACITY IN MILLION LITRES: 2.5

WHAT TO LOOK FOR: Jura 10-, 16- and 21-year-olds; Superstition

Open to visitors

Kilchoman (10)
Bruichladdich, Islay. Tel 01496 850011
www.kilchomandistillery.com
This new distillery will be the eighth one on Islay. It was
established in 2005, as a farm distillery, and is the first to
be built on Islay for 124 years. The first spirit comes of age
in 2009, when the first single malt will be released.
CAPACITY IN MILLION LITRES: New distillery
Open to visitors

Lagavulin (11)
Port Ellen, Islay. Tel 01496 302730
www.malts.com
A neighbour of Laphroaig and Ardbeg, with the sea on the
doorstep, Lagavulin produces heavily peated whisky, but with
a personalised style. Several smuggling bothies merged to
form the distillery in 1817.
CAPACITY IN MILLION LITRES: 1.7
WHAT TO LOOK FOR: Lagavulin 12-year-old Cask Strength;
Lagavulin 16-year-old; Distiller's Edition Double Matured
Open to visitors

Laphroaig (12)
Port Ellen, Islay. Tel 01496 302418   www.laphroaig.com
Pronounced Laff-royg. There's something very fishy going on
here — how about sardine, along with smoke, seaweed and
medicine? This is the most heavily peated of the single
malts, with a third of the barley malted on site, spending
18 hours smoking in peat before drying. Two women have
been in charge here during the 20th century: Catherine
Johnson, the niece of the founder, and Bessie Williamson, a
Glasgow-born secretary, who became indispensable and
inherited the business in 1954.
CAPACITY IN MILLION LITRES: 2.4
WHAT TO LOOK FOR: Laphroaig 10- and 15-year-olds; Laphroaig
10-year-old Cask Strength; Laphroaig Quarter Cask
Open to visitors

Springbank (13)
Campbeltown, Argyll. Tel 01586 552085
www.springbankdistillers.com
This distillery survived the bad times of the 1930s and still
belongs to the Mitchell family who started it. When it
opened in 1828, there were 13 others in the town. The
same Mitchell brothers owned Glengyle but when they fell
out, William moved over to Springbank instead. A true
survivor, Springbank has managed to maintain quality and
concentrate on producing single malts instead of whisky for
blending. It has three stills and concentrates on three single
malts, with varying degrees of peatiness.
CAPACITY IN MILLION LITRES: 2
WHAT TO LOOK FOR: Springbank 10-, 15- and 25-year-olds;
Springbank 10-year-old 100% Proof; Hazelburn Triple
Distilled; Longrow
Open to visitors

Talisker (14)
Carbost, Isle of Skye. Tel 01478 614308 www.malts.com
This is Skye's only surviving distillery: there were once
seven. Founded in 1830, it was a long way from the good-
quality east-coast barley. Grain was delivered by small
steamships which also took away whisky casks, after a quick
float down Loch Harport so that it could be taken on board.
Little is left of the original buildings, following a fire in the
1960s. Until 1928, this spirit was triple distilled. Talisker 18-
year-old was voted Best Malt in the World by *Whisky
Magazine* in 2007.
CAPACITY IN MILLION LITRES: 1.9
WHAT TO LOOK FOR: Talisker 10-, 18- and 25-year-olds; 1986
Distiller's Edition Double Matured
Open to visitors

Tobermory (15)
Tobermory, Isle of Mull. Tel 01688 302645
www.burnstewartdistilleries.com
Opened officially in 1837, but already working in 1797, this is Mull's only distillery. Tobermory was built as a model village, to try to encourage the locals to take up fishing, instead of making moonshine. After varied ownership and shut downs, it was brought back to life in 1993. The whisky, with a clean taste and no oiliness, is matured on the mainland at Deanston.
CAPACITY IN MILLION LITRES: 1
WHAT TO LOOK FOR: Tobermory 10-year-old; Leidaig 10-year-old
Open to visitors

Port Charlotte (16)
Bruichladdich is reopening Port Charlotte Distillery, using equipment from the Inverleven distillery, demolished in 2003, and creating a 'green' distillery with a zero-carbon footprint. The distillery will use the existing warehouses of the former Lochindaal Distillery, which closed in 1929. When a new distillery is built it is usually ten years before there is anything to sell, but Port Charlotte whisky, a heavily peated single malt, has been distilled since 2001, so there will be eight years' worth of stock already in 2009.
CAPACITY IN MILLION LITRES: 1.2
New distillery

CLOSED DISTILLERIES OF THE ISLANDS REGION
Port Ellen

THE LOWLANDS

During the early 1800s, there was a real north-south divide between the Highland and Lowland regions of Scotland. In the south, farming was benefiting from agrarian reforms, such as drainage, use of fertilisers and new crop rotations, whereas in the Highlands things had barely changed. The arable farms of the Lowlands were producing higher yields and distilleries, like that of James Stein at Kilbagie, were consuming more and more barley, wheat and oats. Cheap grain spirit was much in demand in London for rectifying into gin. The laws designed to help the Highlands malt production and prevent smuggling only increased the divide. Farmers and distillers went for quantity rather than quality.

There were, at one point, 200 licenced distillers in the Lowlands, mainly producing malt from pot stills. During the 19th century many distilleries converted to Coffey stills and continuous production of grain whisky. Most of the malt still produced went for blending. Today, there are only three distilleries producing single malt, with a fourth distillery beginning to sell in 2009. Most Lowland malts are light and delicate, with grassy or citrus tones.

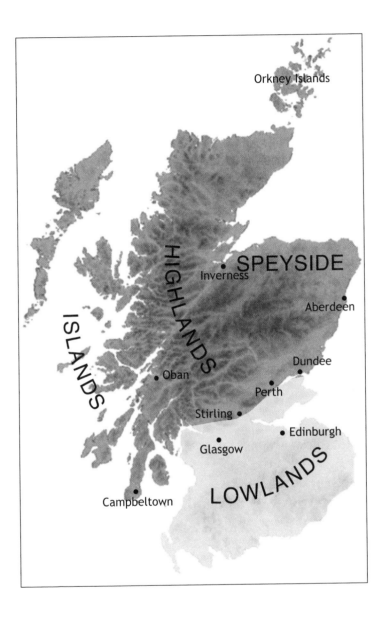

LOWLAND DISTILLERIES

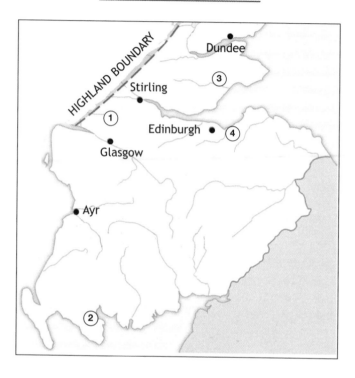

KEY TO MAP
(1) Auchentoshan
(2) Bladnoch
(3) Daftmill
(4) Glenkinchie

Auchentoshan (1)
Clydebank, Glasgow. Tel 01389 878561
www.auchentoshan.com
Situated on the outskirts of Glasgow, the single malt from here is triple distilled and light. The present site was once a monastery, so it may be that the monks turned their hand from brewing beer to making whisky after the Dissolution of 1560. The distillery was licensed in 1823. Sometime after 1878, a third still was added, giving a method similar to the Irish production of whiskey.
CAPACITY IN MILLION LITRES: 1.75
WHAT TO LOOK FOR: Auchentoshan Select; Authentoshan Three Wood; Auchentoshan 10- and 21-year-olds
Open to visitors

Bladnoch (2)
Wigtown, Wigtownshire. Tel 01988 402605
www.bladnoch.co.uk
Said to have been founded in 1817 and kept in the same
family until 1930, Bladnoch has seen several owners since.
This distillery nearly bit the dust when it was bought by a
developer for holiday homes, but, luckily, it was taken out
of mothballs and re-established as a distillery instead.
CAPACITY IN MILLION LITRES: 0.25
WHAT TO LOOK FOR: Bladnoch 10-, 12-, 13- and 15-year-olds
Open to visitors

Daftmill (3)
Cupar, Fife. Tel 01337 830303
www.daftmill.com
This new, farm-based micro-distillery began distillation in
2004, and so the first whisky matured in 2007.
CAPACITY IN MILLION LITRES: New distillery
Open to visitors

Glenkinchie (4)
Pencaitland, Tranent, East Lothian. Tel 01875 342004
www.discovering-distilleries.com
Glenkinchie is close to Edinburgh, and represents the
Lowlands with a good, light, quality whisky. The Museum of
Malt Whisky Production is housed in the old maltings. In the
mid 19th century, it had good barley and water supplies
with a railway running close by, making it easy to supply
Edinburgh's needs. By the 1880s, the boom in Scotch for
blending was well underway and, despite small hold-ups in
production, it has been in business ever since.
CAPACITY IN MILLION LITRES: 1.7
WHAT TO LOOK FOR: Glenkinchie 10-year-old; Distiller's Edition
14-year-old
Open to visitors

CLOSED BUT STILL REMEMBERED

- Glen Flagler
- Inverleven
- Kinclaith
- Ladyburn
- Littlemill
- Rosebank
- St Magdalene

OTHER PLACES TO VISIT

The Museum of Malt
Glenkinchie Distillery, Pencaitland, East Lothian
www.discovering-distilleries.com

The Scotch Whisky Heritage Centre
The Royal Mile, Edinburgh
www.whisky-heritage.co.uk

BLENDED SCOTCH WHISKIES

The following list is a combination of blended whisky
brands which have been recommended from a variety
of sources. I have included supermarket brands,
because that's where a lot of us buy our whisky. The
list is not fully inclusive, because there are so many
brands around and I'm no connoisseur.

100 Pipers
Aberdour Piper
Alistair Graham Scotch Whisky (Sainsbury)
Antiquary
Asda Blended Scotch (Glenmorangie)
Avonside
Ballantine's
Bailie Nicol Jarvie
Bell's Aged 8 Years
Bell's Extra Special
Best 8-year-old Scotch Whisky (Morrison's)
Big T
Black Bottle
Black & White
Buchanan's
Campbeltown Loch
Catto's
Chivas Regal
Clan Campbell
Clan MacGregor
Claymore
Co-operative Group (CWS) Scotch Whisky
Cutty Sark
Dewar's White Label
Duncan Taylor Aged Blend
Dimple
Famous Grouse
Fortnum & Mason 5-year-old
Glen Rossie (Thresher's)
Haig Gold Label

Hankey Bannister
Harrod's Finest Blended Aged 5 Years
High Commissioner
Highland Queen
Isle of Skye 8 Years Old
J&B
John Player Special
Johnnie Walker
Kenmore (Marks and Spencer)
Kings Crest
Lang's
Lauder's
Loch Ranza
Long John
MacArthur's
Mac Na Mara
Majestic Wine Fine Oak Cask Matured Scotch
Old Parr
Old Smuggler
Passport
Pigs Nose
Robert Burns
Royal Salute
Sainsbury's Scotch whisky
Scottish Leader
Something Special
Stewarts Cream of the Barley
Te Bheag
Teacher's Highland Cream
Tesco Value Scotch whisky
The Claymore
VAT 69
Waitrose Scotch 3-year-old
White Heather
White Horse
Whyte & Mackay
William Grant
William Lawson's

OTHER WHISKIES AROUND THE WORLD

IRISH WHISKEY

You might think that, because Scotland probably acquired the skills of distillation from the Irish, Irish whiskey should be just as famous as Scotch, if not more so. Added to that, with Aeneas Coffey hailing from the Emerald Isle, you might expect that Ireland might be famous for an alcoholic drink other than Guinness. A series of somewhat unfortunate events and circumstances, however, made people think otherwise.

For a large part of history, Irish whiskey, rather than Scotch, was the drink of the nobility and the elite. The oldest distillery, Bushmills, in Northern Ireland, received its licence from King James I in 1608.

Irish whiskey was very popular in Britain during the 18th and 19th centuries. In 1779, there were said to be 1,200 distilleries in Ireland, mostly unlicensed. Ireland, however, refused to export whiskey to England, and tried to reduce production through the temperance movement. So, English drinkers turned to Scotland instead. A few families managed to expand their business at the expense of other, smaller producers.

Large quantities were also exported to the West Indies and the US market. It was a combination of the introduction of Scotch blended whisky and the success of Prohibition in the US that crippled Irish whiskey. By the time Prohibition ended, the Irish producers could not produce enough to satisfy the markets and the Scottish industry boomed.

By the 1960s, three of the remaining distilleries joined forces in a new company called the Irish Distillers. In 1975, the new company moved all its production to a new distillery at Midleton, built behind an older one. After a few years, Seagram's had bought both IDL and Bushmills, the last remaining independent distillery in Ireland. More recently, however, there has been renewed interest in Irish whiskey, largely driven by Jameson's.

Irish whiskey is more expensive to make than Scotch, because it is mostly triple distilled, adding about 50% to the bill. Other differences are in malting, where the kilns used to dry the barley don't generally use peat. This is surprising, considering that Ireland is covered in peat bogs. There are only four distilleries producing whiskey today, including one micro-distillery.

IRISH DISTILLERIES

Bushmills
Bushmills, County Antrim.
www.bushmills.com
It has been suggested that whiskey may have been produced in the region as early as 1276. At the end of the 1700s, Bushmills was producing close to 50,000 litres of whiskey, most of which went to the US and the West Indies. The distillery even owned its own ship, to transport the sought-after whiskey across the Atlantic.

As in many Scottish distilleries, the pagoda roof was designed in the late 1800s by the architect Charles Doig, to improve the draught through the kiln.
Bushmills is triple distilled and uses high-quality casks.
Bushmills 16-year-old was named Best Irish Single Malt 2008 by *Whisky Magazine*.

Cooley
Cooley Peninsula, east coast.
www.cooleywhiskey.com
This is an independent distillery, built on the site of a converted potato alcohol plant, which was bought in 1987 and started to produce in 1989. Soon after, Cooley Distillery bought the right to use two dormant whiskey brands, the Kilbeggan and Locke's. The distillery also owns the Tyrconnell Single Malt, Connemara Peated Single Malt, Locke's 8-year-old Single Malt, Kilbeggan, Locke's Blended and Millars Irish whiskey. The Connemara Cask Strength won an award in 2008 from *Whisky Magazine*. Tyrconnell Aged 10 Years Madeira Finish was named Irish Whiskey of the Year by Jim Murray.

Kilbeggan
Kilbeggan, County Westmeath.
This used to be the home of Locke's distillery, which closed in 1953, but distillation began again in 2007. Only the second distillation takes place here, but there are plans for expansion.

Midleton
Midleton, Cork.
www.jamesonwhiskey.com
Old Midleton Distillery was founded in the early
17th century, when Irish whiskey was booming.
It employed 200 people and produced 1.5 million litres
(almost 500,000 gallons) of whiskey a year. This is now a
museum, housing the Jameson Heritage Centre.

In 1975, the new distillery was built by the Irish Distillers
Group. It produces whiskey for four brands: Jameson,
Paddy, Powers Gold Label and Midleton. The distillery also
produces grain whisky. The pot stills and column stills stand
side by side in a very high-tech distillery. Midleton produces
more than 25 spirits.

SOME IRISH WHISKEY NAMES TO LOOK FOR
You need to be careful, as some brands come as
single malts and blends as well, so read the labels
carefully.

Single Malts
Bushmills
Cadenhead
Clontarf
Connemara
Knappogue Castle
Locke's
Magilligan
Michael Collins
The Tyrconnell

Pot still whiskeys
Green Spot
Red Breast

Blends
Black Bush (Bushmills)
Cassidy's Distillers Reserve
Coleraine Blend
Crested Ten (Jameson)

Dunphys
Finnegan
Inishowen Peated Whiskey
Jameson
Kilbeggan
Midleton
Millars Blend
Old Dublin
Paddy
Powers
Tullamore Dew

Single grain
Greenore

PLACES TO VISIT

Tullamore
Bury Quay, Tullamore, County Offaly
www.tullamore-dew.org
This distillery is now a museum.

Old Jameson Distillery
Bow Street Distillery, Smithfield, Dublin
www.oldjamesondistillery.com

Locke's Distillery
Kilbeggan, County Westmeath
www.lockesdistillerymuseum.ie

UK WHISKY VENTURES

Yes, there are distilleries in England and Wales.

There has been talk of new distilleries opening in Northumberland and Cumbria, but there are already three fairly new distilleries up and running.

Penderyn Distillery
Tel 01685 813 300   www.welsh-whisky.co.uk
This distillery in the Brecon Beacons has been producing very successful whisky. The geological significance of the area is recognised by UNESCO and the Fforest Fawr National Park, which surrounds Penderyn. Launched in 2004, it has impressed the experts and commands high prices. A visitor centre opened in 2008.

The Cornish Cyder Company
Penhallow, Newquay, Cornwall
This cider company has been producing whisky for about five years, although the whisky is not yet available. The first casks were set down in February 2002. I was given some mustard with cider vinegar produced by this company recently. What a coincidence!

St George's Distillery
Norfolk, England   www.englishwhisky.co.uk
This family distillery was built from scratch, with equipment and expertise from Scotland. First bottling will take place in late 2009.

EUROPEAN WHISKY DISTILLERIES

Unsurprisingly, other European countries have realised that, with the right geology and water supplies in mountainous areas, they can make whisky as well.

Belgian Owl Distillery
Grace Hollogne, Belgium
www.belgianwhisky.com

Bellerhof Brennerei
Owen, Germany
www.bellerhof-brennerei.com
Schwäbischer Whisky vom Bellerhof.

Blaue Maus Distillery
Eggolsheim-Neuses, Germany
www.fleischmann-whisky.de
Products include Blaue Mause, Krottentaler, Schwarzer and Spinnaker single malts.

Distillerie des Menhirs
Quimper, Brittany, France
www.distillerie.fr
The Celtic influence produces Eddu Gold and other Eddu single malts.

Distillerie Glann ar Mor
North Brittany, France
www.glannarmor.com
The first single malt was produced in 2005.

Distillerie Guillon
Louvois, Reims, France
www.whisky-guillon.com
This distillery is located in the Champagne region, and produces Guillon No 1 single malte de la montage de Reims.

Distillerie Warenghem
Brittany, France
www.whisky-breton.com
Armorik is the name of the single malt.

Domaine Mavela Distillerie Astisanale
Corsica, France
Makes P&M single malt and also blends.

Kaiser's Castle
Elfingen, Switzerland   www.whisky-castle.com

Lantenhammer Distillery
Schliersee, Bavaria
Whisky is bottled as 'Slyrs'.

Mackmyra
Gästrikland, Sweden
www.mackmyra.com
Mackmyra Preludium 05 Svensk Single Malt caused a stir in 2007, and Mackmyra Privus 05 won World's Best Other Single Malt in *Whisky Magazine*'s 2008 awards.

Waldviertler Roggenhof
Kirchschlag, Austria
www.roggenhof.at
Single malts are known by H. Gersten-Malzwhisky and Waltviertler.
Rye malt: Roggen-Malzwhisky.
Rye: H. Feinster-Roggenwhisky.

Weidenauer Distillery
Kottes, Austria
info@weidenauer.at
This distillery makes Waldviertler Haferwhisky oat whisky and spelt (a variety of wheat) whisky.

OTHER EUROPEAN WHISKIES TO TRY
These are for interest only, not a personal
recommendation.

12 Years Finest Bulgarian 43% (Bulgaria)
Ankara Turk Viskisi (Turkey)
Black Horse Ammertal Whiskey Malt and Grain
(Germany)
Castle Hill Whisky (Switzerland)
Dark Whisky (Poland)
Glen Vignettes Swhisky (Switzerland)
LB Lavijas Belzams (Latvia)
Santis Swiss Highlander single malt (Switzerland)
Swissky (Switzerland)

AMERICAN WHISKEY

When George Bernard Shaw described Britain and the
US as 'two countries, separated by a common
language', he could have been referring to any
number of subjects, but his philosophy applies equally
to that of the differences between Scotch whisky and
American whiskey. It isn't just the spelling which is
different, even though the ingredients for both are
grain, water and yeast.

Emigration during the 18th century saw huge numbers
of people from Ireland and Scotland entering America,
bringing with them the skills of the distillery. Since
barley was in short supply, farmers adapted to
growing rye and local corn or maize.

BOURBON
By the end of the American War of Independence in
1784, commercial distilleries had been established in
Kentucky, producing corn-based whiskey with limestone
filtered water. It was called bourbon — after the kings
of France who had helped rebels in the Revolutionary
War — and gained a reputation for quality, as it was

aged in charred oak casks. By 1840, bourbon was recognised as a distinctive American type of whiskey, and spread to several other states. At first it was made in pot stills, but column stills soon took over.

Towards the end of the 19th century, the Temperance Movement grew across America and gained in support. Irish whiskey was popular, outselling Scotch, with over 400 brands being sold in the US. National Prohibition in 1919 had long-standing effects on the bourbon industry, apart from shutting down most of the distilleries. This didn't mean that everyone stopped drinking and there was plenty of illicit alcohol around, as well as imported Canadian whisky which had a lighter taste than bourbon. When Prohibition ended in 1933, many distilleries remained closed, and, by 1990, there were only 10 distilleries left in Kentucky and two in Tennessee.

Today, bourbon is known globally among whisk(e)y drinkers, although this is not the only style of whiskey made in the US. Jim Beam is a popular bourbon. To qualify as bourbon, at least 51% of the grain used for the mash must be maize, and it must be matured for two years in new oak barrels. That's why there are so many bourbon barrels around to be used for Scotch to mature in.

BOURBON DISTILLERIES

I have only listed those distilleries which are open to the public — should you be in the area! A quick trip via the Internet might be a good idea, though, and gives some idea of the range of bourbons available. Bardstown has a bourbon festival every September, if you happen to be on holiday there.

Buffalo Trace
Leestown, Frankfort, Kentucky
www.buffalotrace.com

Brown-Forman/Early Times
Shively, Louisville, Kentucky
www.earlytimes.com

Four Roses
Lawrenceburg, Kentucky
www.fourroses.us

Heaven Hill Bernheim Distillery
Bardstown, Kentucky
www.heavenhill.com
www.bourbonheritagecenter.com

Jim Beam
Boston and Clermont, Kentucky
www.smallbatch.com
Knob Creek is made here.

Woodford Reserve
Versailles, Kentucky
www.woodfordreserve.com

Maker's Mark
Loretto, Kentucky
www.makersmark.com

Wild Turkey
Lawrenceburg, Kentucky
www.wildturkeybourbon.com

TENNESSEE WHISKEY
Tennessee whiskey is a close relative of bourbon, but with an additional step in the production process, called the Lincoln County Process. This entails filtering the spirit through thick beds of maple charcoal, which removes some of the congeners and fats and creates a smooth, mellow taste. The most famous of these is Jack Daniel's.

George Dickel Tennessee Whisky
Normandy, Tennessee
www.dickel.com

Jack Daniels Distillery
Lynchburg, Tennessee
www.jackdaniels.com

RYE WHISKEY

For European immigrants to the US, rye had been the primary grain used in the production of schnapps and vodka in northern Europe. The distilling practice concentrated on Pennsylvania and Maryland, where Rye whiskey remained dominant well into the 20th century, even though rye whiskey was affected more by Prohibition than bourbon. Consumers weaned on relatively delicate spirits turned away from the hard-edged, grainy, full-bodied Rye whiskies. Today, it is used mainly for blending, although Rittenhouse Rye is still a well-known name.

Anchor Distillery
www.anchorbrewing.com

Michter's Distillery
Schaefferstown, Pennsylvania
Information available via www.ellenjaye.com
This site also has information on visits to all the bourbon distilleries.

WHEAT WHISKEY

I have to admit that I had never heard of whiskey made from 51% or more wheat, but it has made a name for itself in recent years. One example is Bernheim Original Straight Wheat Whiskey.

AMERICAN SINGLE MALT
Yes, you did read correctly. There is growing interest in American single malt whiskey, although they are very young still. Some of these are:

Clear Creek Distillery, Portland, Oregon
www.clearcreekdistillery.com
McCarthy's Oregon Single Malt, aged 3 years, 40% abv.

Edgefield Distillery, Portland, Oregon
www.mcmenamins.com
Edgefield Hogshead.

Stranahan's Distillery, Denver, Colorado
www.stranahans.com
Colorado Whiskey, aged 2 years, 47% .

St. James Spirits, Irwindale, California
www.saintjamesspirits.com
Peregrine Rock, 40%.

St George Distillery, Alameda, California
www.stgeorgespirits.com
St George single malt, aged 3 years, 43%.

Anchor Distillery
Makes single malt with rye.

BLENDED AMERICAN WHISKEY
The taste and quality of these whiskies is said to vary according to the ratio of straight whiskey to grain spirit. Early blends were frequently flavoured with all sorts, from sherry to tobacco. They are cheaper and blander in character, and use dozens of different straight whiskeys. Blended American whiskey had a great sales boost during World War II, but sales fell afterwards.

CANADIAN WHISKY

Yes, we're back to English spelling with Canadian whisky. Production of mainly rye-based spirit began in Canada during the mid 19th century, in column stills. During the first half of the 20th century, Hiram Walker and Seagram dominated not only US whiskey but Canadian whisky as well. The blend of different ryes with corn-based spirit is produced using different distillations and spirit runs. A small quantity of other, non-Canadian spirit (around 9%) can also be added to the mix, giving smooth, balanced drinks. This means that Canadian whisky has a reputation for only producing blends for mixing and cocktails, and it is hard to find outside the continent of North America. After a long decline in popularity, however, there is renewed interest. Alberta Premium 25-year-old was commended by *Jim Murray's Whisky Bible Awards* in 2008. In addition, Glenora distillery in Nova Scotia has won the right to market Glen Breton single malt.

Canadian Single Malt
Glenora Distillery, Nova Scotia
Glen Breton Rare
Glenora 1990, aged 14 years, single cask

DISTILLERIES TO VISIT
Not many distilleries appear to be open to visits, and not all have websites.

Alberta Distillers
Calgary, Alberta

Canadian Club Distillery
Walkerville, Windsor, Ontario
www.canadianclubwhisky.com

Gimli Distillery
Manitoba

Highwood Distillery
Alberta
www.highwood-distillers.com

Kittling Ridge Distillery
Grimsby, Ontario
www.kittlingridge.com

The Black Velvet Distilling Company
Alberta
www.bartoninc.com

CANADIAN BLENDED WHISKY BRANDS TO TRY
Alberta Premium
Alberta Springs
Black Velvet
Canadian Club
Centennial
Century Reserve
Crown Royal
Forty Creek
Gibson's
Highwood
Hiram Walker
Mountain Rock
Northern Light
Seagram's
Schenley
Wiser's

JAPANESE WHISKY

Japan has been producing whisky since the 1920s, but has only recently reached world-class status, or so the experts say: you need to go to Japan to find them, so that's a bit of a problem for most of us. Bill Murray seems to have hit on a winner with the product he was advertising in the film *Lost in Translation*, however.

Japanese whisky distillation began because of a chemist called Masataka Taketsura, who went to Scotland, in 1918, to study at Glasgow University and to work at a distillery in Rothes. Even back then the Japanese had a taste for Scotch, it seems, so Taketsura was able to persuade the owners of what became the Suntory Company to produce barley malt and grain whiskies in the same way as in Scotland. They had to import the peat-smoked malted barley from Scotland, but the company was successful. Other distilleries followed, producing single malt and grain whiskies for blends. Today, whisky distilleries are scattered throughout Honshu and Hokkaido, the two main northern islands. The Nikka Whisky Distillery, which was founded by Taketsura in 1934, and Suntory still produce over 80% of Japan's whisky.

Some blind tastings carried out over recent years have resulted in Japanese single malts, particularly those of Yoichi and Yamazaki, scoring higher than their Scotch counterparts. Shock horror!

There are eight Japanese distilleries currently producing single malt whisky.

Websites tend to be difficult to find, or understand.

Chichibu
This distillery opened in 2008, and uses the stocks from the old Hanyu distillery. It markets the Ichiro malt card range, Chichubu (57% abv) and Golden Horse.

Eigashima (website in Japanese)
Until 2007, all of the malt went into White Oak blends. It
has now released an 8-year-old Akashi single malt.

Gotemba, also known as **Kirin**
Produces Fuji-Gotemba Single malts.

Hakushu Higashi Distillery
www.suntory.com
Several Hakushu Single malts are produced. They are mostly
well above 40% abv: some reach 56% or even 63%.

Karuizawa
Owned by Kirin, and founded in 1955, it markets under the
same name.

Miyagikyo (Sendai) Distillery
www.nikkawhisky.co.jp
Look for Miyagikyo and Sendai single malts of over 45% abv.

Yamazaki Distillery, Osaka
www.suntory.com
Opened in 1923, most of the single malts are, again, over
45% abv. Look for Yamazai and Suntory names.

Yoichi Distillery, Hokkaido
www.nikka.com
Opened in 1934, and run by Nikka, the distillery sells Yoichi
and Nikka Whisky Yoichi single malts. Some are over 60%
abv. Yoichi 20-year-old single malt won an award in 2008.

SOME JAPANESE BLENDS TO LOOK OUT FOR

Black Nikka	Imperial
Boston Club	Kakubin
Diamond Whisky	Nikka Whisky
Emblem	Royal
Evermore	Suntory
Golden Horse	Tsuru
Hibiki	White

OTHER WORLD WHISKIES

It is no surprise that countries like Japan and the US have used their natural resources and climate to distil whisky. Commonwealth countries like Canada and New Zealand are also easy to understand, but I have to admit I hadn't put Australia into this category until I thought about Tasmania and its links with Scotland. Rather more surprising are some of the countries below, none of which I ever associated with whisky drinking, let alone making it. Eastern Europe and Asia have increased production as economies develop. The following section just goes to show that you can make whisky anywhere that anyone will drink it.

ARGENTINA
Breeders Choice
Uses Scottish malt and Argentinian grain whisky to make this blend.

AUSTRALIA
Bakery Hill Distillery, Victoria
www.bakeryhilldistillery.com.au
Bakery Hill Malt is a force to be reckoned with.

Booie Range, Queensland
www.booie.com
Booie Range Single Malt.

Hellyers Road Distillery, Tasmania
www.hellyersroaddistillery.com.au
Original Pure Australian Single Malt Whisky is 46.2% abv.

Lark Distillery, Tasmania
www.larkdistillery.com.au
Lark Distillery Single Malt has been recommended.

Tasman Distillery
Great Outback Rare Old Australian Single Malt.

Tasmanian Distillery & Museum, Tasmania
www.tasmaniadistillery.com

Old Hobart and Sullivan's Cove are made here. Sullivan's Cove has won several international awards over the past few years; it also exports whisky.

Small Concern Distillery
Cradle Mountain Pure Tasmanian Malt
Some Cradle Mountain is also vatted with single malt from Springbank, in Scotland.

Nant Distillery, Tasmania
www.nantdistillery.com.au
Nant single malt.

Yalumba Winery
www.singlemalt.com.au
Smith's Angaston Whisky Vintage comes from here, the home of Barossa Valley wine.

BRAZIL
Brazil? Well, there are a lot of European ex-pats there.

Single malts are represented by Durfee Hall Malt, (Heublein Distillery) and Barrilete (Union Distillery). See www.celticmalts.com for some information on the latter.

Blends
Cockland Gold
Green Valley
Natu Nobilis
Malte Barrilete
O Monge
Old Eight
Pitt's

INDIA
There's no problem associating whisky with India, given the 300 years of British involvement.

Amrut Distilleries
www.amrutdistilleries.com

Amrut Single Malt and Amrut Cask Strength (62% plus abv) are fairly well known and appreciated by many.

Ponda Distillery
Makes Stillman's Dram Single Malt, 42.8% abv.

Indian blends
Antiquity
Blenders Pride
Peter Scot
Royal Challenge
Royal Stag
Signature

NEW ZEALAND

The Southern Distilling Company Ltd
www.hokonuiwhiskey.com
The Coaster Single Malt and The MacKenzie Blended Malt are made here.

Wilson Distillery
www.maltexo.co.nz
This distillery made the Milford Aged range as well as Lammerlaw and Cadenhead's ranges. It closed in 2000 but now brews on another site as Wilson Distillers.

SOUTH AFRICA

James Sedgwick Distillery
www.celticmalts.com

Makes Three Ships 10-Year-Old and the following blends:
Harrier
Knights
Three Ships Bourbon Cask Finish

HOW TO ENJOY DRINKING WHISKY

HOW TO ENJOY DRINKING WHISKY

I was amused to note, when watching *Harry Potter and the Goblet of Fire* on TV the other day, that the visiting head teacher character, played by Frances de la Tour, insisted that her horses only drank single malt whisky. That might pose a few problems. What if they didn't all appreciate the Islay malts, or preferred a Speyside? They certainly wouldn't go for White Horse either!

Some people will need no encouragement to drink whisky and will enjoy the experience no end, without help, but there is a particular way of going about it if you are trying to experience more than the feeling of the spirit trickling or burning down your throat when you have a cold. Like tasting wine, there is a method. Of course, how you drink whisky is entirely up to you.

DO YOU NEED GLASSES?
I always thought that you should drink whisky from a wide-mouthed tumbler, possibly a cut-glass one. My husband and I had a set given as a wedding present in the 1970s, even though neither of us was a whisky drinker, but this was obviously something to aspire to. They were there to pull out of the sideboard when we had visitors, even though we didn't have the whisky to go in them. Nowadays, we are told that a whisky glass should be shaped like an elongated red wine glass, or even to use the wine glasses instead. This is good news, since we have only one whisky tumbler left after 35 years and numerous moves!

THE EYES HAVE IT
Before you put the glass to your lips, hold on a minute. You can tell a lot about the whisky by the colour, which can be anything between pale straw and dark, chocolaty brown. You can test the strength of alcohol by shaking the bottle (closed). Bubbles appear. Strong whisky has small bubbles which last

longer and standard whisky, at 40% abv, has bigger bubbles which quickly disappear. Pour some whisky into the glass and swirl it around. Traces will run down the sides and these can also tell you something about the age of the whisky. Slow thick traces show that the whisky is old.

The colour tells you more about the cask the spirit was matured in. That kept in bourbon will be golden-yellow, whereas sherry-matured whisky will be amber to rich brown. A darker colour can be due to age, although this is not always a reliable indicator: bourbon casks will always give a lighter colour, and older bourbon cask matured single malt will always be lighter than newer whisky from a sherry cask. Another factor is that an older cask which has been used before will not give as much colour as one which has been used for the first time.

NOSE TO THE LEFT — OR RIGHT
Assuming you are still reading and haven't given up and swigged the contents of the glass, let's continue. After swirling the whisky around, smell it from a distance, then bring it closer to your nose. Proceed with care; strong whiskies can make your eyes water and your nose prickle. You can either smell with both nostrils at once or with either left or right. I go for the one nostril technique, and my nose is still twitching from smelling some blended whisky five minutes ago, but I always knew I was a wimp. I have the same problem with red wine, so, if I sneeze, that's the tasting out of the window (or into the spittoon!). I'm told that people smell the most extraordinary things in single malts, if they have the right olfactory glands and sinuses. How about roast beef and Yorkshire pudding, lemons, Christmas pudding, oranges, ginger or kippers? Some of us are just nasally challenged. Some people can smell better when the whisky is diluted with water, but taste it first, if you can.

TASTING

Go on, don't just sip it — have a good mouthful and roll it around your mouth and over your tongue. Then let the taste spread down your throat and right down to your toes. You might be able to assess whether the taste is rich or thin, zesty or cloying. The taste may linger after you have swallowed. This is called the finish. A finish of kipper might not be a good thing. Obviously, the most important thing is whether you like the taste and smell, rather than that someone tells you that what you just tasted has won stacks of awards or that an expert tells you it is good. I understand that only too well, living for some of the year in the Côtes de Bourg region of the Bordeaux wines. There are some really good wines and some pretty bad ones, but some people find the 'good' ones too oaky and variable, year on year. They still prefer an Australian red which is more consistent and perhaps less complex. Like wines, some people will always prefer the latter or a blended whisky.

You don't have to drink it neat either. My dad always drank his daily measure with tap water. Others prefer a dash of soda water or even lemonade, ginger ale or Orangina. If this is the case, it would seem a shame to spend more on a single malt, when a blend will do. I can't recommend mixing an Islay malt with coke either!

If you are really keen, you can find out more about tasting sessions. Here are some more contact details:

The Scotch Malt Whisky Society www.smws.com and follow 'tastings'.
You can go on a whisky tasting course.
www.scotchwhisky.com
Visit a distillery or go on a tour.
www.scotlandwhisky.com

WHISKY LIQUEURS

I've noticed that whisky liqueurs don't feature in whisk(e)y books generally. I can understand why, but since this is not a book for connoisseurs, I've included them in the drinks section.

If you prefer alcoholic drinks which are quite sweet and infused with additional flavours, then whisky-based liqueurs may be for you. They are said to smooth off the edges and reduce the pronounced alcohol taste of whisky, just like alcopops. The spirit can be infused or re-distilled with herbs, fruit, honey, cream, nuts or spices.

Some contain up to 70% abv, so are a bit of a nightmare regarding units of alcohol.

The most popular in the UK are probably Baileys Irish Cream and Drambuie. Liqueurs can be distilled from any type of whisk(e)y. Here is a list of some others from around the world.

Arran Gold Whisky Cream Liqueur
Atholl Brose contains Benromach Speyside single malt and herbs.
Baileys Irish Cream is made from Irish whiskey and Irish cream. The Bushmills equivalent is no longer made.
Cock O the North, made with Speyside single malt whisky and blaeberries (Scottish blueberries).
Columba Cream Single Malt Whisky Honey and Cream Liqueur. This liqueur was inspired by the 6th century St Columbas, and originally contained oats.
Compass Box Orangerie is made with sweet, 10-year-old Scotch whisky infused with fresh orange peels and spices. I must try this one, as it is said to be excellent when you drink it with fine chocolate.

Drumgray Cream Liqueur
Eblana, made from Irish whiskey, coffee, honey, almonds and peanuts.
Drambuie was said to be the favourite recipe of Bonnie Prince Charlie. Whiskies, including 15–17-year-old malts, are blended with heather honey and a still-secret recipe of herbs and spices.
Glayva started in Leith and is based on honey, spices and herbs. Glayva means 'very good' in Gaelic.
Glenfiddich Whisky Liqueur, made from single malt, infused with spices and honey.
Heather Cream
Hebridean Whisky Liqueur
High Peak Liqueur
Irish Mist Whiskey Liqueur
Johnnie Walker Liqueur
Lochan Ora Whisky Liqueur, made from aged Chivas Regal, blended with heather honey and herbs. Very sweet and exceptionally smooth.
Old Pulteney, prunes and spices with a single malt whiskey.
Original Lakeland Liqueur
Rock and Rye Whiskey Liqueur, rye whiskey with citrus and rock candy.
Scottish Island Liqueur
Southern Comfort Whisky Liqueur (70% abv)
Stag's Breath Whisky Liqueur is lower in alcoholic strength and drier on the palate. It is made from Speyside blended whiskies and fermented honeycomb.
The Famous Grouse Liqueur, blended whiskies, infused with citrus spices.
Wallace Whisky Liqueur, created using Deanston Highland single malt mixed with traditional berries and French herbs.
William Shakespeare Whisky Liqueur
Yukon Jack Whiskey Liqueur, honey-based Canadian liqueur.
Zuidam Liqueur is made in the Netherlands, from Scotch whisky and honey.

POPULAR COCKTAILS AND DRINKS

I'm not a great drinker of spirits myself, let alone cocktails. If you feel inclined to try some of these recipes, please stick to the measures and enjoy the experience. One cocktail can put you over the daily recommended limit quite easily. Generally, one measure is about 40 ml (1½ fl oz).

RUSTY NAIL

Use equal parts of Scotch and Drambuie. Mix and serve with ice.

WHISKY MAC

I always thought of this as a cold or sore throat remedy, but it makes a warming drink, especially in the depths of winter, in front of a roaring fire.

    35 ml (1½ fl oz) whisky
    25 ml (1 fl oz) ginger wine

Directions
Mix together, gargle (if your throat's sore) and enjoy.

HIGHLAND SLING

    2 teaspoons of water
    1 teaspoon sugar
    55 ml (2 fl oz) Scotch whisky
    25 ml (1 fl oz) lemon juice
    Lemon twist
    Ice

Directions
Mix the water and sugar first, then add the rest of the liquids. Shake well and pour over ice cubes, garnishing with the lemon twist.

FLYING SCOTSMAN

Mix equal measures of Scotch and vermouth with a dash of bitters and a few grains of sugar. Shake well with crushed ice, then strain and serve.

SCOTCH HORSE'S NECK

This must be for two or more to share. Don't attempt to get on a horse after one of them either!

2 parts Scotch
2 parts vermouth
2 parts Italian vermouth
2 dashes Angostura bitters
Ginger ale
Thinly peeled lemon skin
Ice

Directions
Mix together the spirits and bitters. Put ice into the glass with the lemon peel. Pour over the spirits and top up with ginger ale. Find a safe place to sit before you fall over.

WHISKY HONEY CREAM

Another of those sweet, creamy drinks I can't take to.

2 parts blended whisky
1 part double cream
1 part honey syrup
Ice

Directions
Mix together and pour over the crushed ice.

GINGER WHISKEY COOLER

Make honey syrup by mixing 4 parts honey to 1 part hot water. Cool before use. If, like me, you find this too sweet, reduce the honey.

   1 shot whisky
   ½ shot Cointreau
   2 parts honey syrup (*see above*)
   1 part iced tea
   1 part ginger ale
   2 lemon wedges
   Ice

Directions
Build this in a tall glass over ice cubes.

WHITE KNIGHT

This is not my cup of tea, but someone may like to try it. 15ml is equivalent to one tablespoon.

   35 ml (1½ fl oz) Bailey's Irish Cream
   15 ml (½ fl oz) Irish whiskey
   15 ml (½ fl oz) coconut rum
   35 ml (1½ fl oz) single cream
   Crushed ice

Directions
Mix all of the ingredients in a cocktail shaker with ice. Pour into a short glass to serve.

DEPTH CHARGE

This sounds fun, assuming you've got the right sized glasses. If not, I suppose you just have to pour the whiskey into the beer.

Directions
Fill a tall glass ¾ full of beer. Pour 35 ml (1½ fl oz) Canadian whiskey into a shot glass. Drop the shot glass into the glass of beer and drink them together.

SAZERAC

55 ml (2 fl oz) rye whiskey
½ teaspoon white sugar
Dash of Peychaud bitters
Dash of Angostura bitters
15 ml (½ fl oz) Pernod
2 ice cubes
Lemon slice

Directions
Combine the rye and sugar in a short glass containing the ice cubes. Add the remaining liquid ingredients and stir well. Garnish with a lemon slice.

MANHATTAN

35 ml (1½ fl oz) bourbon
20 ml (¾ fl oz) sweet vermouth
Ice
Cherry for garnish

Directions
Shake the spirits and ice together and pour into a cocktail or short glass. Garnish with the cherry.

WHISKY SOUR

35 ml (1½ fl oz) blended whiskey
25 ml (1 fl oz) lemon juice
½ teaspoon sugar
Crushed ice

Directions
Fill a short glass with ice. Shake the other contents together and strain into the glass.

IRISH WHISKEY MOJITO

35 ml (1½ fl oz) Irish whiskey
100 ml (4 fl oz) cranberry juice
½ teaspoon sugar
12 mint leaves, crushed but not chopped
Juice of half a lime
Lime wedge for garnish

Directions
Mix the sugar with the whiskey, cranberry juice and lime juice. Put the ice and mint leaves into a tall glass and pour over the liquids. Serve with swizzle stick and lime wedge.

BOURBON SATIN

35 ml (1½ fl oz) Bourbon whiskey
20 ml (1 fl oz) single cream
20 ml (1 fl oz) White Creme de Cacao

Directions
Shake with ice and pour into a chilled cocktail glass.

PEAT TREAT

This recipe suggests using peated whisky, but I'll leave the choice up to you.

    35 ml (1½ fl oz) peated whisky
    20 ml (¾ fl oz) Poire William liqueur
    100 ml (4 fl oz) apple juice
    Sprig of rosemary
    Grated cinnamon
    Cinnamon stick
    Ice

Directions
Shake together the liquids and grated cinnamon. Pour over ice cubes and garnish with rosemary and cinnamon swizzle stick.

BOURBON PUNCH

This American punch serves a multitude and certainly packs one. You could always reduce the quantities.

    100 ml (4 fl oz) Amaretto
    1 bottle bourbon whiskey
    1.5 litres (3 pints) cold coffee
    500 ml (1 pint) single cream
    1 litre (2 pints) ice cream, vanilla or coffee
    Grated plain chocolate for garnish

Directions
Mix all of the ingredients in a large bowl. Garnish with plain chocolate shavings.

HOT DRINKS

HOT TODDY

This traditional drink will give any cold or flu symptoms a hammering, and helps you sleep well too.

- 1 part whisky
- 1 part honey
- 1 part lemon juice
- 3 parts boiling water

Directions
Stir the honey and lemon juice into the hot water. Allow it to cool slightly before adding the whisky.

GAELIC COFFEE

Joseph Sheridan, the head chef at what is now Shannon Airport, is credited with serving this drink in the early 1940s. Irish actor and musician Alex Levine once quipped that it has all the essential food groups in a single glass: alcohol, caffeine, sugar and fat. The only difference between Gaelic Coffee, Irish or Clansman's Coffee is the type of alcohol used for flavouring.

CLANSMAN'S COFFEE

This is a version of Gaelic coffee, with an aniseed twist.

- 25 ml (1 fl oz) Scotch whisky
- 20 ml (¾ fl oz) Sambuca
- Strong black coffee (hot)
- Whipped cream or double cream
- Brown sugar to taste

Directions
Wet the rim of a tall, warmed glass and dip into the sugar. Put the whisky and Sambuca into the glass and carefully pour in the coffee. Add sugar, as required, and stir well. Top with whipped cream or spoon double cream, lightly whipped, over the coffee to make it float. Drink the coffee through the cream.

DRAMBUIE COFFEE

3 dessertspoons Drambuie liqueur
1 level dessertspoon light brown sugar
Fresh, strong coffee
Double cream

Directions
Warm the glass. Add the Drambuie and stir in the sugar. Pour in the coffee, leaving 2.5 cm (1 in) below the rim. Keep stirring until the sugar has dissolved and pour in the cream over the back of a teaspoon so that it floats on the surface to a depth of about 1 cm ($1/2$ in).

GAELIC COFFEE

Black coffee, freshly made
Scotch or Irish whiskey
Demerara sugar
Double cream, whipped until slightly thick

Directions
Follow the method above.

ROB ROY

½ measure Scotch
½ measure dry vermouth
Dash of Angostura bitters

Directions
Mix well and drink with or without ice.

EARTHQUAKE

I can quite see where this one got its name from!

1 measure gin
1 measure Scotch
1 measure anis (Pernod or Ricard)

Did the earth move for you?
As they say, enjoy alcohol sensibly!

POSSIBLE EFFECTS TO HEALTH FROM DRINKING WHISKY

'Taken sanely and in moderation whisky is beneficial, aids digestion, helps throw off colds, megrims and influenzas. Used improperly the effect is just as bad as stuffing on too many starchy foods, taking no exercise, or disliking our neighbor.'

CHARLES H. BAKER, JR,
THE GENTLEMAN'S COMPANION, 1939

Can there possibly be any health benefits? Millions of consumers think there are. There is a suggestion that moderate consumption of single malt can help to reduce the risk of cancer or heart disease. Whisky contains ellagic acid, an antioxidant, which is found in numerous fruits and vegetables including raspberries, grapes, walnuts, pecans and pomegranates. The highest levels are found in cranberries, grapes and strawberries.

There has been a lot of talk about red wine being beneficial to health when taken in moderation, backed up by research into the antioxidants it contains. But now we are told that there may be even greater benefits from drinking single malt. Wouldn't that be convenient? Apparently, single malt contains more ellagic acid than red wine, although the benefits seem to be associated with low consumption of alcohol. Mind you, we could get the benefits of ellagic acid by drinking fruit juice or eating the fruit instead, but perhaps that wouldn't be so exciting.

Moderate drinking is associated with better health and longer life than either abstaining entirely or abusing alcohol by over consumption, and medical researchers have based this on scientific evidence.

These findings don't include pregnant women, people who have difficulty controlling their drinking, or anyone with a medical condition where abstinence is recommended. Some groups, such as menopausal women and men over the age of 40 who may be prone to heart trouble, are likely to get more benefit from moderate whisky consumption. My dad had a small whisky and water every day before lunch for years, on medical grounds.

A study carried out in Aberdeen tested the effects of a large shot of whisky containing 3—4 standard measures taken once a week. This study was partly sponsored by the drinks industry. It compared the effects of drinking mature single malt (12-year-old) with newly made malt and red wine, on an empty stomach. Over three weeks, each participant tried the three drinks and levels of phenols were tested. Findings showed that both mature whisky and red wine raised the body's levels of antioxidants, although the effects were short-lived. More phenols were absorbed from the mature whisky than the red wine, although the red wine contained more phenols originally. The newly made whisky didn't have the same effect, possibly because of the copper in the new whisky.

WHAT IS MODERATE CONSUMPTION?
The recommended daily consumption is:
• No more than 2—3 units for women
• No more than 3—4 units for men

That sounds straightforward enough, until you start to think of the various sized glasses for wine there are around today. We were given some as a present which contain about half a bottle each. They are still in the box!

HOW MUCH IS A UNIT?
That also depends on the alcoholic drink and also the

specific amount of alcohol by volume (abv) in any brand. Half a pint of (4%) beer accounts for about 1 unit. A whole pint of (5%) beer or cider contains 3 units. Wines vary in strength quite a lot, but will normally be between 10% and 14%. A small glass of wine containing 125 ml will have 1.25 to 1.5 units of alcohol. A standard glass of wine (175 ml) will contain 1.75 to 2.1 units and a bottle contains 7.5 to 9 units.

A 70 cl bottle of whisky contains 28 units of alcohol, so one unit is only 25 ml of single malt at 40% abv. A small measure of whisky is set at 25 ml and a large measure is 35 ml (1.4 units). The chances are, if you are drinking at home, that the measure will be a lot more generous than that. So there you are — I hope that cleared up the question!

As a matter of interest, binge drinking has been defined as consuming double the daily recommended units. I guess that we can all easily come into that category from time to time, so bingeing can, apparently, happen to the best of us, in that case. Consuming alcohol in moderation does reduce the risk of heart disease. It also significantly reduces the risk of stroke, unless there are other medical complications. Drinking too much can increase the risk of developing cancers of the mouth, throat, oesophagus, liver and bowel.

Alcohol is absorbed through the stomach and small intestine. From here it enters the bloodstream and is quickly distributed throughout the body, reaching the heart, brain, muscles and other tissues. The liver gets rid of the alcohol, which cannot be stored, and changes the alcohol from toxic substances, eventually, into harmless ones. Then it is excreted through urine, breath and sweat. This process, apart from putting a strain on the liver, dehydrates you and causes a hangover to the unlucky ones.

RECIPES
USING
WHISKY

PEPPERED CHICKEN WITH WHISKY CREAM SAUCE

This recipe works just as well using quorn pieces, as a vegetarian option.

You will need   Serves 4

    4 boneless chicken breasts, skinned
    2 tablespoons black peppercorns, crushed
    salt
    1 tablespoon oil
    25 g (1 oz) butter
    2 shallots or small onions, finely chopped
    100 g (4 oz) mushrooms, sliced
    50 ml (2 fl oz) whisky
    175 ml (6 fl oz) cream or crème fraiche
    1 tablespoon chopped chives

Method

1. Coat the chicken breasts with the crushed pepper and salt. Heat the oil in a large frying pan with the butter and add the chicken breasts. Cook on each side for three to four minutes, or until cooked thoroughly, then remove and keep warm.
2. Add the finely chopped shallots or onions and sliced mushrooms to the pan and brown them. Simmer until soft. Return the chicken to the pan and add the whisky, chives and cream (or crème fraiche).
3. Serve immediately.

BOURBON CHICKEN WITH PINEAPPLE

You will need   Serves 4

    3—4 skinless, boneless chicken breasts, cut into
        small pieces
    2 cloves garlic, crushed
    1 teaspoon freshly grated ginger
    1 tablespoon oil soy sauce
    450 ml (16 fl oz) pineapple juice
    90 ml (3½ fl oz) bourbon whiskey
    Ground black pepper

Method
1. Heat the oil in a large pan over medium heat and sauté the chicken with the garlic and ginger until cooked through.
2. In a small bowl, combine the soy sauce, pineapple juice, bourbon and pepper. Pour over the chicken and let simmer for 10 to 15 minutes, until the sauce is thickened to taste.

BEEF IN WHISKY SAUCE

You will need   Serves 4–5
    1 tablespoon melted butter
    700 g (1½ lb) sirloin steak cut into strips
    1 onion, finely chopped
    3 tablespoons Drambuie
    3 tablespoons double cream
    Salt and pepper

Method
1. Put the butter into a pan and add the beef strips. and onion. Cook for 4–5 minutes, stirring occasionally.
2. Stir in the Drambuie and cream and season to taste. Heat gently, but don't allow it to boil.
3. Serve with green beans.

PANCAKES WITH WHISKY AND ORANGE SAUCE

The pancakes for this delicious dessert can be made ahead and the sauce added at the last minute before reheating.

For the pancake batter   Serves 4
    125 g (4 oz) flour
    1 egg, beaten
    300 ml (10 fl oz) skimmed milk
    1 tablespoon oil
For the sauce
    80 g (3 oz) butter
    100 g (4 oz) sugar
    Juice of 3 freshly squeezed oranges
    Grated zest of 1 orange
    Grated zest and juice of 2 lemons
    3 tablespoons whisky

Method

1. Put the flour in a large bowl and make a well in the middle. Add the beaten egg and gradually stir in half the milk and the oil. Beat until smooth and add the rest of the milk.

2. Heat a medium-sized frying pan and add a few drops of oil. Pour in a tablespoon of the batter and tilt the pan to coat the bottom thinly but evenly. Cook until brown and then turn and cook for another 10 seconds. Place on a warmed plate while you make the rest of the pancakes.

3. Fold each pancake into quarters and arrange them in a shallow, heat-proof dish

4. To make the sauce, melt the butter and stir in the sugar until dissolved. Add the fruit juice and zest. When simmering, add the whisky.

5. Pour the sauce over the pancakes and put into a preheated oven for 10 minutes at 170°C (325°F, gas mark 3). The pancakes will absorb a lot of the sauce. Delicious!

CHOCOLATE AND WHISKY CREAM MACAROON DESSERTS

These are quick to make and will happily sit in the fridge until required.

You will need   **Serves 4**

    8 macaroon biscuits
    2 tablespoons whisky or whisky liqueur
    50 g (2 oz) butter
    50 g (2 oz) caster sugar
    75 ml (3 fl oz) milk
    225 g (8 oz) chocolate

Method

1. Place four of the macaroons in the bottom of the serving dishes, and drizzle the whisky over the top.

2. Cream the butter and sugar together. Boil the milk and allow to cool for 10 minutes.

3. Put the chocolate, broken into pieces, in a bowl over a pan of hot water to melt. Add to the milk with the butter and sugar. Beat until smooth.

4. Pour half of the sauce into the dishes, add another macaroon and top up with the remaining sauce.

5. Refrigerate for 12 hours before serving.

MOCHA WHISKY CREAM

This very adult dessert certainly got the thumbs up from friends. I used 99% cocoa solid chocolate, which was too bitter to eat from the bar, even for me. The result was a very chocolaty, not overly sweet coffee chocolate sensation, with a twist. You can use crème fraiche instead of whipping cream if you like

You will need   **Serves 4**
  150 g (5 oz) good-quality chocolate (at least 70% cocoa butter)
  2 tablespoons strong black coffee, sweetened or not, to taste
  1 tablespoon whisky
  3 eggs, separated
  125 ml (5 fl oz) whipping cream

Method
1. Break the chocolate into a basin with the coffee over a pan of warm water, until the chocolate melts. Remove from the heat and add the whisky.
2. Beat in the egg yolks, one at a time.
3. Whisk the egg whites and then the cream. Fold these into the chocolate mix.
4. Pour into dishes and chill for one hour.

MOUSSE AU CHOCOLAT

The benefit of this version is that there are no eggs involved.

You will need   **Serves 4**
  200 ml (7 fl oz) water
  100 g (4 oz) castor sugar
  100 g (4 oz) plain chocolate, grated
  2 tablespoons whisky
  300 ml (10 fl oz) whipping cream

Method
1. Put the water, sugar and chocolate into a saucepan and heat gently until the sugar has dissolved and the chocolate has melted. Remove from the heat, add the whisky and allow to cool.

2. Whip the cream and add most to the chocolate mix. Fold together and pour into serving dishes. Chill thoroughly before serving, garnished with a swirl of cream and chocolate flakes.

BAKED SCOTCH APPLES

These are easy to prepare, delicious to eat and don't contain any fat — unless you serve them with cream.

You will need   **Serves 4**
   4 whole cooking apples, cored
   2 tablespoons water
   80 g (3 oz) dried figs, dates or raisins
   2 tablespoons Scotch whisky
   1 tablespoon honey

Method
1. Make a cut around the middle of each cored apple, but don't peel them. The peel will help to retain the shape. Place in an ovenproof dish with the water.
2. Push the dried fruit into the centres of the apples and pour in the whisky and honey.
3. Bake at 180°C (350°F, gas mark 4) for 45—55 minutes, until soft.

APPLE MERINGUE PIE

For the pastry
   100 g (4 oz) plain flour
   Pinch of salt
   25 g (1 oz) margarine
   25 g (1 oz) vegetable oil
   1 tablespoon water
For the filling
   450 g (1 lb) apples, peeled and cored
   1 tablespoon water
   1 tablespoon honey
   1 tablespoon whisky
For the meringue
   2 egg whites
   100 g (4 oz) sugar

Method
1. Preheat the oven to 200°C (400°F, gas mark 6).
2. Sift the flour and salt into a bowl and rub in the fats to a breadcrumb consistency. Mix in enough water to form a dough. Turn out onto a floured board and roll out. Line an 18-cm (7-in) flan ring or cake tin, and bake blind for 10 minutes. Lower the temperature of the oven to 170°C (325°F, gas mark 3).
3. Meanwhile, prepare the apples by roughly chopping them in a saucepan and adding the water and honey. Cook gently until they soften, and remove from the heat. Add the whisky and stir well to break up the apples and distribute the whisky.
4. Spread the apple mix over the pastry case.
5. For the meringue, whisk the egg whites until stiff. Add half of the sugar and whisk again. Add the remaining sugar, folding it in carefully.
6. Spread the meringue on top of the filling in the case and bake for 25 minutes, until the meringue is crispy and just turning brown. Serve hot or cold.

LEMON WHISKY SYLLABUB

This is one of those desserts you can make early and then forget about until you want to eat it.

You will need   Serves 4
    1 large lemon
    150 ml (5 fl oz) white wine
    50 g (2 oz) caster sugar
    2 tablespoons whisky
    275 ml (10 fl oz) whipping or double cream
    Lemon slices to garnish

Method
1. Grate the zest from the rind and squeeze the juice from the lemon. Put into a bowl with the wine, sugar and whisky. Stir well.
2. Whip the cream and fold in the liquids. Spoon into glasses and refrigerate until needed. Garnish with lemon slices.

DUNDEE CAKE

This not-so-rich fruit cake was popular at the end of the 19th century. If you want to ice the cake, don't put the whole almonds on the top.

You will need
- 225 g (8 oz) plain flour
- 150 g (5 oz) butter
- 150 g (5 oz) granulated or soft brown sugar
- 3 eggs
- 2 tablespoons ground almonds
- 50 g (2 oz) mixed peel, finely chopped
- 175 g (6 oz) currants
- 175 g (6 oz) sultanas
- 100 g (4 oz) glace cherries, washed and halved
- Grated rind of 1 lemon
- Grated rind of 1 orange
- 1 level teaspoon baking powder
- 3 tablespoons blended whisky
- 1 tablespoon milk, if necessary
- 100 g (4 oz) blanched almonds (whole), optional
- 3—4 tablespoons single malt whisky, for feeding the cake after cooking

Method
1. The day before cooking the cake, put the fruit and peel in a bowl with 3 tablespoons of whisky. Leave overnight.
2. Grease and line a 20 cm (8 in) round deep cake tin or an 18-cm (7-in) square one and preheat the oven to 170°C (325°F, gas mark 3).
3. Beat the butter and sugar together until light and fluffy. Whisk the eggs and add them to the mixture, one at a time, beating well.
4. Sift the flour and baking powder and fold into the mix with a large spoon. Add some milk if the batter is too stiff.
5. Fold in the ground almonds and fruit, peel and citrus rind.
6. Fold into the prepared tin and arrange the whole almonds on the top so that they don't sink in. Place in the centre of the oven and cook for 2—2 ½ hours, or until the centre springs back up if pressed down. Leave the cake in the tin to cool for about half an hour, and then turn out onto a wire tray until cold.

7. Pour the whisky over the top of the cake to feed it, and then wrap in baking paper and foil to mature until required. You can feed it again if you are really keen on whisky, or can spare another glass of the single malt, but don't drive immediately after eating this cake!

A SHORT GLOSSARY OF WHISK(E)Y TERMS

abv (alcohol by volume)
The percentage of alcohol in a liquid. Scotch must be at least 40% abv, but can be more.

Age
On a label, this means the number of years the youngest whisky in the bottle spent in a cask. All Scotch whisky must be at least three years old. Some of the whisky may be considerably older.

Angel's share
This is the name given to the whisky which evaporates from a cask during maturation. Usually around 2% a year is lost. This is why cask whisky needs to be stronger than 40% abv.

Blended malt whisky
A mix of vatted malt whiskies from different distilleries.

Blended whisky
A mixture of malt whisky and grain whisky.

Bourbon
American whiskey made from at least 51% maize, distilled to a maximum of 80% abv and matured in new oak barrels for at least two years.

Cask strength
The spirit is originally filled with 63.5% abv and will lose strength. Before it is bottled it is diluted to 40% abv.

Chill filtering
Filtering whisky at a low temperature to prevent cloudiness from impurities or congeners (see page 157).

Condenser
A series of copper tubes and an outer shell through which cold water runs, to turn alcoholic vapours back to liquid. All distilleries use them except where a worm (see page 158) is still in use.

Continuous distillation
Also known as the Coffey still, Patent still and Column still, this is the process by which grain whisky is made.

Congeners
Organic chemical impurities in the spirit, some of which are poisonous or taste bad.

Draff
Grains that remain after mashing. They are dried and used to feed cattle as they don't contain any alcohol. Drunk cattle or whiskied milk are amusing ideas, though.

Dram
Originally this was an 18th-century measure of about a third of a pint of whisky at 60% abv. Nowadays, it is used to describe a tot of whisky.

Feints
The heavy, undesirable spirits which come through the spirit still and are removed, last of all, by the second distillation.

Floor maltings
The traditional way of malting barley, by spreading it over a stone floor to germinate.

Foreshots
The lightest of the unwanted spirits, driven off first by the second distillation.

Grist
Grain which has been roughly ground to a consistency between porridge and flour.

Low wines
The product of the first distillation, coming off the wash still at about 25% abv.

Malt
Barley which has been germinated and then dried to stop it growing.

Mash
A mix of grist and hot water which dissolves fermentable sugars.

Mash tun
A large tank, originally made of wood but now often from stainless steel, where mashing takes place.

Middle cut
The part of the spirit which is kept for making whisky, in-between the foreshots and the feints.

Nosing
A way of assessing whisky by smelling it rather than tasting it.

Pot still
A large copper kettle which distils malt whisky, one batch at a time. These come in different shapes and sizes, which affect the taste of the whisky.

Proof
The traditional way of measuring alcoholic strength, now called alcohol by volume (abv).

Rye whisky
Whiskey produced with at least 51% rye in the mash.

Single malt whisky
Malt whisky which is made using only yeast, malted barley and water, from a single distillery.

Spirit still
The second still in the process of making spirit, where the low wines are re-distilled to achieve around 68% abv.

Wash
The product of adding yeast to the mash or wort, also known sometimes as beer. The strength is about 7–8% abv.

Worm
The traditional method of condensing alcoholic vapour, using a coiled copper pipe coming off the still.

Worm tub
A large tank containing the worm which has cold water pumped in continuously to condense the spirit inside.

Wort
See mash.

Yeast
A type of mould. Living cells feed on fermentable sugars, converting them into alcohol and carbon dioxide.

FURTHER INFORMATION

ORGANISATIONS

The Scotch Whisky Association
20 Atholl Crescent
Edinburgh
EH3 8HF
Tel 0131 222 9200
www.scotch-whisky.org.uk

The Scotch Malt Whisky Association
The Vaults
87 Giles Street
Edinburgh
EH6 6BZ
Tel 0131 554 3451
www.smwa.com

PUBLICATIONS

Whisky Magazine
St Faith's House
Mountergate
Norwich
NR1 1PY
Tel 01603 633808
www.whiskymag.com

Jim Murray's Whisky Bible 2008
All you could ever want to know about any whisky worth drinking!

WEBSITES

Use these websites to find out about events, courses and other organisations devoted to whisk(e)y:

www.scotchwhisky.net

Spirit of Speyside Whisky Festival
www.spiritofspeyside.com

WHISKY

Scotland's Malt whisky Trail
www.maltwhiskytrail.com

Peat Freak — Single Malt Site
www.peatfreak.com

Malt Madness — Single Malt Site
www.maltmadness.com

Whisky Live — Various Locations
www.whiskylive.com

Visiting Distilleries
www.visitingdistilleries.com

Undiscovered Scotland
www.undiscoveredscotland.co.uk

Scottish Tourist Board
www.visitscotland.com

The Malt Advocate
www.maltadvocate.com

The Whisky Portal
www.whiskyportal.com

Celtic Malts
www.celticmalts.com

Whisky Websites
www.whiskywebsites.co.uk

Planet Whiskies
www.planetwhiskies.com